THE
TEMPLE

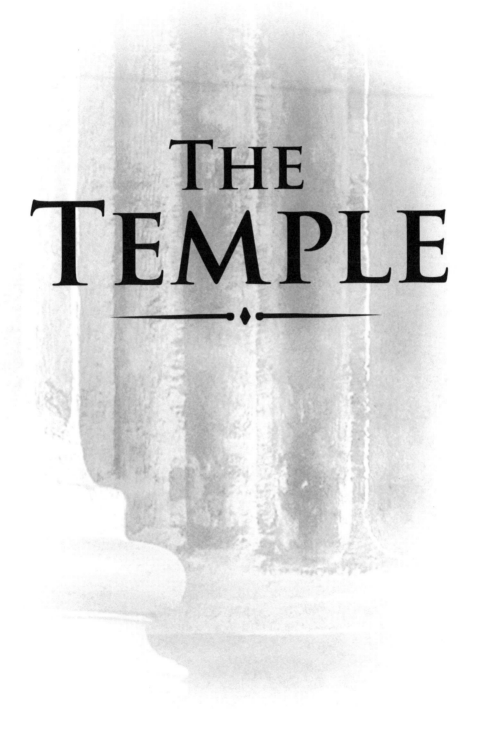

THE
TEMPLE

❦

JIMMY SWAGGART

JIMMY SWAGGART MINISTRIES
P.O. Box 262550 | Baton Rouge, Louisiana 70826-2550
www.jsm.org

ISBN 978-1-941403-38-9

09-145 | COPYRIGHT © 2017 Jimmy Swaggart Ministries®

17 18 19 20 21 22 23 24 25 26 / CM / 10 9 8 7 6 5 4 3 2 1

TABLE OF CONTENTS

INTRODUCTION

GENERAL FLOOR PLAN OF SOLOMON'S TEMPLE

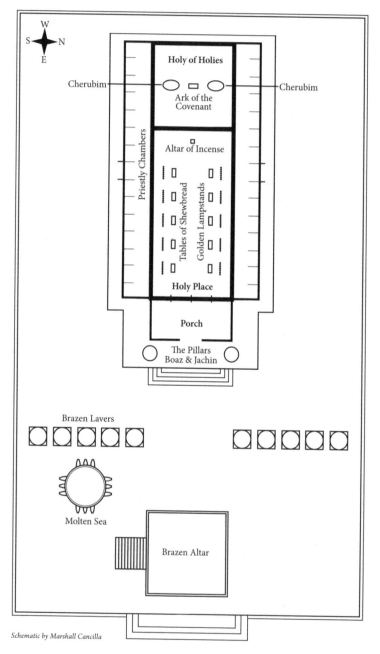

Schematic by Marshall Cancilla

INTRODUCTION

IN BIBLE TYPOLOGY, the tabernacle—the design of which was given to Moses by the Lord—represented redemption. Consequently, it was moved at times, which, in a sense, signified the growth of the believer.

However, the temple—the design of which was given to David but was built by his son Solomon—represented the coming kingdom age. During the time of Solomon, Israel was engaged in very little warfare. Peace reigned, which again typified the coming kingdom age. As well, the temple was stationary (as would be obvious), meaning that it never was moved.

SYMBOLIZING CHRIST

As the tabernacle symbolized Christ in His redemptive work, likewise, the temple symbolized Christ in His finished work. Anything that helps us to learn more about Christ is valuable indeed, and I believe our study of the temple will do just that!

While we will go into detail concerning the construction of the temple, in other words, the way that God demanded that it be built, we will not deal directly, at least to any degree, with the multitudinous functions of the priests, etc. But yet, I think that our study on the most expensive building ever constructed, and the only building per se in which God actually dwelt, will convey what we're trying to do, which is to give a great portrayal of the work of Christ.

OF GREAT SIGNIFICANCE

Anything that the Lord does, and I mean anything, is extremely worthwhile for our study. To be sure, it was God who designed the temple from the proverbial A to the proverbial Z. In fact, neither David nor Solomon contributed anything toward the design or the manner of construction.

The Muslim Dome of the Rock is situated on the temple site at present, but in the coming kingdom age, the millennial temple will be built there. In a sense, it will be occupied by the Lord Jesus Christ. Actually, it was most probably the Holy Spirit, the third member of the Godhead, who occupied Solomon's temple. Due to the Cross, the Holy Spirit now resides in the heart and life of every believer.

Let me walk blessed Lord,
In the way Thou has gone,
Leading straight to the land above;
Giving cheer everywhere,
To the sad and the lone,
Fill my way every day with love.

Keep me close to the side,
Of my Saviour and guide,
Let me never in darkness rove;
Keep my path free from wrath,
And my soul satisfied,
Fill my way every day with love.

Soon the race will be o'er,
And I'll travel no more,
But abide in my home above;
Let me sing blessed King,
All the way to the shore,
Fill my way every day with love.

ALL THAT IS IN
YOUR HEART

ALL THAT IS IN YOUR HEART

"NOW IT CAME TO PASS, as David sat in his house, that David said to Nathan the prophet, Lo, I dwell in an house of cedars, but the ark of the covenant of the LORD remains under curtains. Then Nathan said unto David, Do all that is in your heart; for God is with you" (I Chron. 17:1-2).

THE HEART OF DAVID

David is here as a type of the Lord Jesus Christ residing in Jerusalem in the glories of the coming kingdom age. All enemies are defeated.

David desired to build a house for the Lord. This presents the beginning of the kingdom age when the Lord Jesus, as a *"greater than Solomon,"* will begin to build His house.

While the Lord definitely was with David, it was not the will of God that David build the house, even though it was definitely the will of God for the house to be built. So, what David felt was definitely from the Lord, but he assumed that the Lord wanted him to build the house. He was wrong in that.

The Lord definitely was with David, but, for any number of reasons, it was not the will of God that David build the house. In fact, it would be built by his son Solomon. This tells us that irrespective of whom the person might be, even a prophet such as Nathan, we must not assume that we know altogether what God wants. We must seek His face about everything, which Nathan at that moment did not do, at least when he gave his first answer to David.

THE COMING KINGDOM AGE

Everything pertaining to the temple speaks of the coming kingdom age, which will portray God's glory. The tabernacle portrayed God's grace, and the temple portrayed God's glory; therefore, at that particular time, the tabernacle would have been separated from the ark of the covenant, with the tabernacle residing at Gibeon and the ark residing in Jerusalem. Both David and Solomon were types of Christ. David subduing all of his enemies, casting the Jebusites out of Zion, and setting up there the throne of Jehovah are types of the Messiah when He will come back to this earth and overthrow the Antichrist. In fact, the Messiah is stated in Exodus, Chapter 15, to be Jehovah, the man of war. In Revelation, Chapter 19, it states that He makes war righteously. As the great captain of the host, He will overcome all His enemies, establish His throne in Zion, redeem Israel, and make the Gentiles subject to His scepter. Having accomplished all of this, as the divine Solomon, He will then display the glory of His millennial reign. The building of the temple was designed to symbolize that glory. The tabernacle given to Moses in the wilderness foretold the first advent of Christ in humility; the temple of Solomon foretold His second advent in power and great glory, hence, the grandeur of the temple.

David could not build that temple, for he typified Messiah as a man of war destroying His enemies and setting up His throne.

Solomon, typifying Christ as the Prince of Peace, which he did, built the glorious palace of Jehovah. In doing so, he gave a forepicture of the time when the kingdoms of this world shall become the kingdom of our Lord and of His Christ, the Son of David, who shall reign forever and forever.

TYPES OF CHRIST

David's heart was to build a structure for the ark. To be sure, the Lord most definitely did place it in the heart of David that this structure be built, but, as stated, it was not to be built by the "*sweet singer of Israel.*"

Why?

The temple that would house the ark was a type of the coming kingdom age when Christ will reign supremely in peace, with the world then knowing prosperity and freedom as it has never known before. To be sure, that day is just ahead, but the rapture of the church and the great tribulation must precede this coming event.

At any rate, the temple was to portray that coming grand time, a time of such glory and splendor as to defy all description. Though David was a type of Christ, and perhaps one of the greatest types who ever existed, still, he could not portray Christ in this posture. As we have stated, David was a type of Christ as it regarded redemption's plan, which pertained to the defeat of Satan and all his cohorts (Col. 2:14-15).

As such, David was not a man of peace, even as he could not be a man of peace.

SOLOMON

Solomon, David's son by Bath-sheba, would be a type of Christ as it regarded peace, thereby, the coming kingdom age. In fact, under Solomon, Israel knew peace and prosperity as the nation had not known before and would not know again, at least until the second advent of Christ, which is in the future.

So, we have in both David and Solomon types of Christ, with the former portraying the redemption plan that was purchased at great cost, and the latter as a victory that is totally won. David was a type of the conquering Christ, while Solomon was a type of the victorious Christ. In other words, all victory is now won. So, David could not build the temple, and for the obvious reasons, but he was given the plans in totality, which we shall see.

PROPHETS AND APOSTLES

Concerning the construction of the temple, the Scripture says, "Then Nathan said unto David, Do all that is in your heart; for God is with you."

Now, without fanfare and without introduction, we have Nathan the prophet who comes on the scene.

Under Old Testament guidelines, the prophet, in effect, was used by the Lord to guide Israel. Presently, the office of the prophet is used of the Lord very similarly to Old Testament times, with one great exception. Now, the apostle and not the prophet is the titular leader of the church. This office was inaugurated by the Saviour in the choosing of 12 apostles who would be witnesses of His life, ministry, death, and resurrection, as well as His ascension. While there could never be another 12 like those originally chosen by Christ, with Matthias taking the place of Judas, still, this office is set firmly in the church, meaning that the Lord is still appointing apostles. Counting the Twelve, there were approximately 24 named as such in the New Testament (Eph. 4:11-14).

WHAT ARE THE EARMARKS OF AN APOSTLE

In the Greek, the word *apostle* is *apostolos* and means "a messenger, he that is sent." It actually refers to one sent with a particular message. In fact, a particular message is the greatest earmark of the apostle.

What do we mean by that?

The Holy Spirit, knowing what the church needs, will lay it on the heart of a man (there is no record of a woman being called to be an apostle) to stress a particular message, whatever that message might be. Of course, it will always coincide perfectly with the Word of God, not deviating at all from that Word.

All of this means that apostles aren't appointed by men, aren't selected by men, and aren't voted in on a popular ballot by men. The fact remains that men have absolutely nothing to do with those whom God calls for such an office. As stated, these are the titular leaders of the church, whether recognized as such or not.

TO EMPHASIZE THE MESSAGE

As the Lord sees that the church needs healing, prophecy, faith, or the Message of the Cross emphasized, the Holy Spirit will then appoint certain ones to emphasize the message desired. As well, there could be two or more emphases at the same time. Yet, and I think history will prove me correct, there will always be a greater emphasis on one aspect of the ministry and the work of God.

We see this greater emphasis in the book of Acts and the Epistles as it regards the Cross of Christ. While the Holy Spirit also emphasized other things, this was the primary emphasis of that time, and the Apostle Paul was the titular leader as it regarded that particular message. As well, if it is to be noticed, other than the original Twelve, most of the apostles of that time fell into that category. In other words, their emphasis also was the Cross of Christ.

Down through history, the Lord has emphasized other things. For instance, during the time of Martin Luther, the Lord emphasized justification by faith. At the turn of the 20TH century, the Holy Spirit was emphasized, and rightly so.

At approximately the midtime of the 20TH century, divine healing was emphasized. Now, I believe it is the Message of the Cross.

COUNTERFEITS

To be sure, during the time of the early church, Satan endeavored to hinder the true Message of the Cross—in essence, the message of grace—by attempting to institute the message of law. In fact, this was Paul's greatest nemesis. False apostles from Jerusalem and elsewhere were continually trying to overthrow the message of grace and, thereby, substitute law. Inasmuch as flesh appeals to flesh, they were successful at times.

Presently, false apostles are attempting to institute other types of emphases, such as the Purpose Driven life scheme, the confession message, or the seeker sensitive message. However, as Satan did not succeed in the early church, he will not succeed presently.

Yes, he will draw many aside after these false apostles, whom Paul referred to as *"grievous wolves"* (Acts 20:29). However, for those who truly love the Lord and who truly hunger and thirst after righteousness, the great Message of the Cross, which is the present emphasis by the Holy Spirit, will be paramount (Acts 20:29-30).

PRESUMPTION

We should take a lesson from this which Nathan said to David. Both were great men of God; however, Nathan was wrong in telling David to *"do all that is in your heart."* Neither one had prayed about the matter. They were presuming this was what the Lord wanted; however, presumption is never the thing to do.

We must pray about everything, whether it's little or large. God is omniscient, meaning that He knows all things, past, present, and future. We, as human beings, are very much limited. We know very little about the past, very little about the present, and very little, if anything, about the future. So, we need to pray about everything and ask the Lord's leading and guidance, never presuming that we know what He wants and desires. The example given us here proclaims the fact that even the godliest cannot know what the Lord wants without ardently seeking His face. Let us say it again because it is so very, very important. We must never presume that we know what the Lord wants. We must seek His face about everything, and to be sure, He has a perfect will as it regards every single thing, whether it be small or large. God's ways are right, and they are right not simply because they are His ways, but because they *are* right. He knows the way through the wilderness, but we don't!

GOD'S UNCONDITIONAL COVENANT WITH ISRAEL

And it came to pass the same night, that the Word of God came to Nathan, saying, Go and tell David My servant, Thus says the LORD, you shall not build me an house to dwell in: For I have not dwelt in an house since the day that I brought up

Israel unto this day; but have gone from tent to tent, and from one tabernacle to another. Wheresoever I have walked with all Israel, spoke I a word to any of the judges of Israel, whom I commanded to feed My people, saying, Why have you not built Me an house of cedars? Now therefore thus shall you say unto My servant David, Thus says the LORD of Hosts, I took you from the sheepcote, even from following the sheep, that you should be ruler over My people Israel: And I have been with you wheresoever you have walked, and have cut off all your enemies from before you, and have made you a name like the name of the great men who are in the earth. Also I will ordain a place for my people Israel, and will plant them, and they shall dwell in their place, and shall be moved no more; neither shall the children of wickedness waste them anymore, as at the beginning, And since the time that I commanded judges to be over My people Israel. Moreover I will subdue all your enemies. Furthermore I tell you that the LORD will build you an house (I Chron. 17:3-10).

THE BLESSING OF THE COVENANT

As to how the Lord spoke to Nathan, we aren't told; however, the main thing is that Nathan was in such a spiritual condition that God could speak to him. Regrettably, that isn't the case with most.

The Hebrew marks the personal pronoun *you* in verse 4 as emphatic; *you* shall not build.

In verse 5, the Lord reminds David how surely and faithfully he has shared the pilgrim lot and unsettledness of His people.

Verse 7 records the price of admission into this house. It is trust in the slain lamb by the route of humility. As well, David was a shepherd, and the Lord Jesus Christ also would be a shepherd (Heb. 13:20).

Verse 9 proclaims God's unconditional covenant with Israel; however, it must be stated that this unconditional covenant is unconditional only in the sense that God will bring the promises to pass irrespective. The only thing that is unconditional is the covenant itself. To come into the blessing of the covenant, one must meet its conditions, which are faith in Christ and what Christ has done at the Cross. Those Jews who do this will definitely dwell in the place ordained for them, which is the land of Israel. This includes all Jews who have accepted Christ before death and all those who will accept Him at the second coming.

The more complete fulfillment of this great promise awaits the coming of the Messiah (Isa. 9:6-7; Rom. 11:25-27).

A PLACE FOR ISRAEL

What did the Lord mean when He spoke to David saying, *"I tell you that the Lord will build you an house?"*

As we have already stated, while a house most definitely was to be built, David was not the one who would build it. Emphatically, the Lord stated, *"… you shall not build Me an house to dwell in."*

The idea of verses 5 and 6 is that the Lord had suffered whatever dwelling He had. We speak of the time during the wilderness, as well as the time of the judges and through the reign of Saul.

The idea is that Israel was very unsettled during that time. They had little sense of purpose or direction, a time frame, incidentally, which lasted several hundreds of years. So, to epitomize Israel's condition during that time, the ark of the covenant was moved *"from tent to tent"* and *"from one tabernacle to another."* In other words, whatever it was, in which the ark of the covenant was placed, was indicative of what Israel was at that time. For most of that particular time, Israel was out of the will of God. In fact, the time frame of the judges is fraught with rebellion against the Lord. And then, they jumped the gun, demanding a king when it was not time, and the result was Saul. Basically, they treated the ark of God with disdain simply because they were not functioning correctly; they were not functioning in the will of God; and they were not functioning as believers should function.

WHAT TYPE OF HOUSE DOES
THE LORD HAVE NOW?

We should take a lesson from this. When you came to Christ, the Holy Spirit came into your heart and life to abide permanently (Jn. 14:16). Concerning this, Paul said: *"Know you not that you are the temple of God (where the Holy Spirit abides), and that the Spirit of God dwells in you?"* (I Cor. 3:16) (The Expositor's Study Bible).

Is the temple in which He abides obedient? Is it subservient to the Lord? Is it, God forbid, filled with pollution?

The Lord didn't leave Israel during those times of acute failure, and neither will He leave you; however, as is His dwelling place, so will you be!

It must be understood that the modern believer cannot make a fit house for the Lord without his faith being entirely in Christ and what Christ has done at the Cross. That sounds like a simple statement and, in fact, it is; however, that simple statement, faith in Christ and what He did for us at the Cross, exclusively lays waste all of man's concoctions, schemes, efforts, and futile plans. Man doesn't like that, so it is not easy for him to fully accept the Message of the Cross. However, if the believer is to have a proper house in which the Holy Spirit is to dwell, he can do so only by his faith in Christ and the Cross (Rom. 6:1-14; 8:1-11; I Cor. 1:17-18, 23; 2:2; Gal., Chpt. 5; 6:14; Eph. 2:13-18; Col. 2:14-15).

THE SHEPHERD

As we have stated, although David failed miserably at times, still, he was a type of Christ. Perhaps as a shepherd, his type did show greater than all. Jesus was and is the Great Shepherd—the Great Shepherd of the sheep. In fact, David learned how to be a *"ruler over My people, over Israel"* (II Sam. 7:8) by being a shepherd. The Lord made David a name by linking the name of Christ to David. In fact, our Lord would be referred to as the son of David, and there could be no higher honor shown to David, or any human being for that matter, than that of which we speak. Nothing is greater than being linked to Christ!

What kind of house would the Lord build David? This house would be his link to Christ. It will finally be realized in the coming kingdom age when Israel will at last accept Jesus as

Saviour, Messiah, Lord, and Master. Then, this house of Israel will function under Christ as it was always intended to be. While the kingdom was offered to Israel at the first advent of Christ, as is obvious, they rejected it. They wanted the kingdom, but they didn't want the king, i.e., the Lord Jesus Christ. In fact, millions today want the kingdom, but they don't want the king. Let the following be understood:

It is impossible to have the kingdom, or any part of the kingdom, unless one first of all has the king, and that king is the Lord Jesus Christ.

The truth is, we don't build the Lord much of anything. He builds us a house.

THE BUILDING OF THE HOUSE

The major problem with believers is that we try to build the house, which, in fact, we cannot do. Actually, it is impossible! And yet, the house must be built. Abraham tried to build the house through Ishmael. Jacob tried to build the house through his schemes. In fact, all of us have tried to build this house and found to our dismay that we were unable to do so. If the house is to be built, the Lord must build it. What do I mean by building the house?

I mean that we try to build righteousness and holiness within our hearts and lives. We try to effect our spiritual growth by our religious machinations. However, let it ever be understood that religious flesh is still flesh and is totally unacceptable to God (Rom. 8:8).

The believer cannot build his own house. In other words, he cannot make himself righteous or holy, no matter what he does. We cannot effect the growth of the fruit of the Spirit. Actually, as it regards living for God, i.e., building this house, we cannot do anything except provide to the Lord a willing mind and an obedient heart. The Lord alone can build the house.

How does He do such?

He does it by us placing our faith simply, clearly, and completely in Christ and the Cross, which then gives the Holy Spirit latitude to work within our lives, thereby, building the house (Rom. 8:1-11; Col. 2:10-15). Otherwise, it will be built on sand and will topple with the first difficulty that arises.

FOREVER

And it shall come to pass, when your days be expired that you must go to be with your fathers, that I will raise up your seed after you, which shall be of your sons; and I will establish his kingdom. He shall build Me an house, and I will establish his throne forever. I will be his father, and he shall be My son: and I will not take My mercy away from him, as I took it from him who was before you: But I will settle him in My house and in My kingdom forever: and his throne shall be established forevermore. According to all these words, and according to all this vision, so did Nathan speak unto David (I Chron. 17:11-15).

Verse 11 has a double application. Solomon was spoken of in the immediate present, but far more so, the Lord Jesus

Christ as the *"Son of David."* As it regards the building of the house as described in verse 12, the total fulfillment will be in Christ, who will occupy this throne in the coming kingdom age and then forever.

The Muslims should read the words of verse 14 and consider them carefully. In fact, the entirety of the world needs to read them and consider them carefully.

SPIRITUAL CONSTRUCTION

While the Lord alone can build the house, the facts are, He uses human instrumentation to do so. The Scripture says: *"Except the* LORD *build the house, they labor in vain who build it"* (Ps. 127:1).

In fact, in the building of this house (the single most important thing in the history of man), which pertains to the incarnation of our Lord, the Lord is the One who chose the family through which the Redeemer would come. It would be the family of David. Through his line, which would be an unfailing line of descendants, the Messiah would ultimately come. This verse 11 is probably that to which Peter referred in his statement of Acts 2:29-30.

While the first part of verse 11 refers to David, the latter part refers to his son, Solomon. In fact, the lineage of David followed all the way to Christ, which it was intended to do. Mary went back to David in her lineage through Nathan, another son of David. Joseph went back to David through Solomon, so the lineage of Christ was perfect in every respect, just as here promised.

The phrase in verse 14, *"And his throne shall be established forevermore,"* in effect, has a double meaning. Most of all, it refers to Christ who will occupy this throne *"forevermore."* The scriptural indication is that David will reign upon this throne under Christ and, in essence, will do so forever.

THE PRAYER OF DAVID

And David the king came and sat before the Lord, and said, Who am I, O LORD God, and what is my house, that You have brought me hitherto? And yet this was a small thing in Your eyes, O God; for You have also spoken of Your servant's house for a great while to come, and have regarded me according to the estate of a man of high degree, O LORD God. What can David speak more to you for the honor of Your servant? for You know Your servant. O LORD, for Your servant's sake, and according to Your own heart, have you done all this greatness, in making known all these great things. O LORD, there is none like You, neither is there any God beside You, according to all that we have heard with our ears. And what one nation in the earth is like Your people Israel, whom God went to redeem to be His own people, to make You a name of greatness and ter-ribleness, by driving out nations from before Your people, whom You have redeemed out of Egypt? For Your people Israel did You make Your own people forever; and You, LORD, became their God. Therefore now, LORD, let the thing that You have spoken concerning Your servant and concerning his house be established forever, and do as You have said. Let it even be

*established, that Your name may be magnified forever, saying,
The* LORD *of Hosts is the God of Israel, even a God to Israel:
and let the house of David Your servant be established before
You. For You, O my God, have told Your servant that You will
build him an house: therefore Your servant has found in his
heart to pray before You. And now,* LORD, *You are God, and
have promised this goodness unto Your servant: Now therefore
let it please You to bless the house of Your servant, that it may
be before You forever: for You bless, O* LORD, *and it shall be
blessed forever* (I Chron. 17:16-27).

THE MANNER OF MAN

David now knew fully and beyond the shadow of a doubt
that the Messiah would come through his lineage. Even though
it is not recorded in this chapter, still, in II Samuel 7:19, David
says, *"And is this the manner of man, O* LORD *God?"* This refers to
the promise that the seed of the woman shall bruise the serpent's
head (Gen. 3:15); that is, from David's line the Messiah would
come, bringing eternal salvation and reigning as the eternal king
of the earth. This would be the highest honor that God could
show any man, i.e., high degree.

Verse 18 proclaims the fact that David in no way could merit
this great and high honor, even as no child of God can merit
the high honor of salvation, which is freely given by the Lord
Jesus Christ.

Once again, David exclaimed the glory of God, which is
so much greater than what he had first thought. He wanted to

build a house for the Lord; instead, the Lord told David that He would build him a house, and it would be eternal.

Israel constituted the only people on earth who knew Jehovah, the Creator of the ages. The establishment of this house forever has only been partially fulfilled to date, but it definitely will be fulfilled in the coming kingdom age.

As it regards verse 24, Jesus would say to the woman at Jacob's well, *"For salvation is of the Jews"* (Jn. 4:22). It was through Israel that Jesus, the Saviour of the world, came! When prayers are found in the heart, they are the result of gratitude or the overflow of some desperate need. God keeps His promises! In verse 27, the Lord pronounces Israel *"blessed forever."* This means that Israel will ultimately be restored. It also means that what God has blessed, nothing can curse (Num. 23:8, 20).

THE INCARNATION OF CHRIST

In a sense, what the Lord had spoken to David was beyond comprehension. The remainder of this chapter records his response. And yet, his answer also records the fact that he little understood the implication of that which had been given to him, and neither would we have. For a man to be redeemed, God would have to become man simply because that which was required was beyond the pale of man's ability. So, if redemption were to be brought forth, which would be by the Cross, God would have to become man and carry out this great work Himself.

Angels could not do this thing because they were of another creation, and man couldn't do so simply because of his fallen and polluted condition. God would have to carry out the act, and in order to do so, He would have to become man. In effect, He would become the *"last Adam,"* or as Paul also stated, the *"second man"* (I Cor. 15:45-47). This was done for the purpose of going to the Cross. As well, a perfect sacrifice had to be offered, and God alone could provide such, which He did, in the form of His Son and our Saviour, the Lord Jesus Christ.

GOD IS NOT A MAN THAT HE SHOULD LIE

This is the reason that man is so foolish when he attempts to place Christ in the category of a mere man. While Jesus most definitely was a man in every respect, still, He was not only a man, He was, as well, God! One might say that He was the God-man, the Lord Jesus Christ. All of this means that He was very man and very God. He was God manifest in the flesh. Concerning all of this, Paul said:

> *For what the law could not do, in that it was weak through the flesh* (those under law had only their willpower, which is woefully insufficient; so despite how hard they tried, they were unable to keep the law then, and the same inability persists presently; any person who tries to live for God by a system of laws is doomed to failure because the Holy Spirit will not function in that capacity), *God sending His own Son* (refers to man's helpless condition, unable to save himself and unable to keep even a simple law and, therefore, in dire need of a Saviour) *in the likeness of sinful flesh* (this means

that Christ was really human, conformed in appearance to flesh, which is characterized by sin, but yet, on His part, sinless), *and for sin* (to atone for sin, to destroy its power, and to save and sanctify its victims), *condemned sin in the flesh* (Jesus destroyed the power of sin by giving His perfect body as a sacrifice for sin, which made it possible for sin to be defeated in our flesh; it was all through the Cross) (Rom. 8:3) (The Expositor's Study Bible).

BLESSED FOREVER

Concerning Israel, emphatically and even dogmatically, the Holy Spirit through David says, *"O LORD, and it shall be blessed forever."* As stated, all of this means that the Lord will ultimately and eventually restore Israel. In fact, this will be done at the second coming, which will be the most cataclysmic event the world has ever known. Then Israel will understand that the one they crucified was and is their Messiah. They will then accept Him and then be restored to their rightful place and position in the family of nations.

In fact, in that coming day, the kingdom age, Israel will be the greatest nation on the face of the earth, and it will all be under Christ.

So, the Muslim world has about as much chance of destroying Israel as Muhammad has of getting out of hell, where he presently is and ever shall be. Something that is blessed may have difficulties and problems but, to be sure, that which the Lord has promised most definitely will come to pass without fail.

O for a thousand tongues to sing,
My great Redeemer's praise,
The glories of my God and king,
The triumphs of His grace.

My gracious Master and my God,
Assist me to proclaim,
To spread through all the earth abroad,
The honors of Your name.

Jesus! The name that charms our fears,
That bids our sorrows cease;
'Tis music in the sinner's ears,
'Tis life and health, and peace.

He breaks the power of canceled sin,
He sets the prisoner free;
His blood can make the foulest clean;
His blood availed for me.

Hear Him you deaf; His praise you dumb,
Your loosened tongues employ;
You blind, behold your Saviour come;
And leap, you lame, for joy.

CHAPTER 2

DAVID

CHAPTER TWO
DAVID

"NOW AFTER THIS IT came to pass, that David smote the Philistines, and subdued them, and took Gath and her towns out of the hand of the Philistines. And he smote Moab; and the Moabites became David's servants, and brought gifts. And David smote Hadarezer king of Zobah unto Hamath, as he went to stablish his dominion by the river Euphrates. And David took from him a thousand chariots, and seven thousand horsemen, and twenty thousand footmen: David also houghed all the chariot horses, but reserved of them an hundred chariots. And when the Syrians of Damascus came to help Hadarezer king of Zobah, David killed of the Syrians two and twenty thousand men. Then David put garrisons in Syria-damascus; and the Syrians became David's servants, and brought gifts. Thus the LORD preserved David whithersoever he went. And David took the shields of gold that were on the servants of Hadarezer, and brought them to Jerusalem. Likewise from Tibhath, and from Chun, cities of Hadarezer, brought David very much brass, wherewith Solomon made the brazen sea, and the pillars, and the vessels of brass" (I Chron. 18:1-8).

NOW IT WILL BE USED FOR GOD

Verses 1 and 2 illustrate the moral fact, which is always true, that when Christ is set upon the throne of the heart, victory over both inward and outward enemies is assured. However, the inward is always first conquered, as in the case of David and the Philistines in this chapter, and then the outward will be conquered.

Hadarezer of verse 3 means "my demon helper"; so, despite demon spirits helping this man, David, who was greater, smote them.

The river Euphrates was the northeastern extremity of the kingdom promised to Abraham by the Lord (Gen. 15:18). Through our "heavenly David," the Lord Jesus Christ, we can conquer and, in fact, must conquer every part of our inheritance. Verse 4 proclaims the fact that Israel's strength was not chariots, but rather the Lord! All of this is a type of Christ, who defeated every enemy at the Cross (Col. 2:14-15). When our faith and trust are placed exclusively in Him and the Cross, His victory then becomes our victory. It is the will of God, and even the insistence of the Lord, that we subdue not just some of our spiritual enemies, but all. We must rule the sin nature, or else, the sin nature will rule us (Rom. 6:3-14).

The wealth of Zobah was illustrated by the shields of gold. Now this wealth belonged to the people of God, stipulating the coming kingdom age.

All of this material of verse 8 that was formerly used for heathen idols would now be used for God as it regarded the building of the temple. This symbolizes the believer who is brought out of sin and darkness, is brought to the family of God, and is made to be *"a pillar in the temple of my God"* (Rev. 3:12).

THE INWARD AND OUTWARD ENEMIES

This chapter is freighted with victory and the reasons such victories are afforded. With Christ as a type of the ark now being enthroned in Zion, the center of the kingdom, David soon enjoyed complete victory over all enemies, both at home and foreign. The Philistines, who were internal enemies, were first bridled, and then, the external foes were brought into subjection. However, before the external foes can be defeated, the internal foes must be defeated, here illustrated by the Philistines. They were within the sacred borders of Israel.

How many Christians still have Philistines within their lives? This is a question that should be looked at very carefully simply because this is so very, very important. External foes, whatever these foes might be, can never be defeated until the inward enemies are subdued. As it regards the modern believer, I speak of uncontrollable temper, jealousy, envy, malice, unforgiveness, and immorality of various stripes, plus many things we haven't named. These are described as inward hindrances, and great hindrances at that, of our Christian walk.

If it is to be noticed, the very first thing that David did when he became king of Israel was to subdue the Jebusites, who occupied the very area where the temple would be built years later. This was in the very heart of Israel and most certainly constituted an inward foe (II Sam. 5:6-10). Then he conquered the Philistines, another inward foe (II Sam. 5:17-25). We will now find that the outward foes—those outside the borders of Israel but promised by the Lord to Israel—would now be subdued.

This lesson must not be lost on us!

THE MANNER OF VICTORY

Without exception, the believer will find that the greatest foes of all are those which are inward foes. Satan knows that if he can keep his strongholds within our hearts and lives, this will greatly hinder our walk and progress with the Lord. So, these things, whatever they might be, must be defeated. There is only one way they can be defeated. Now, understand that, read those words carefully, and believe what is said.

Satan will also come up with every type of means and ways that one can think to overcome these foes, and he will use preachers and entire denominations to carry out his work. However, no matter how religious it might be, there is only one way that victory can be assured in one's heart and life, and that is the way of the Cross. The answer is found in the Cross. The solution is found in the Cross, and the answer and the solution are found only in the Cross! Now, understand that. There is no victory over sin outside of the Cross! There is no victory over inward foes or outward foes outside of the Cross! There is no victory over the world, the flesh, and the Devil outside of the Cross. That is God's way, and a way we might quickly add, that is stamped on every page of the Bible. So, there is no excuse for us to misunderstand.

SO-CALLED SOLUTIONS

Unfortunately, at this particular time, and I speak of the modern church, the Devil is very slickly parading his wares of so-called solutions, which is all propagated by the church. Too many believers have itching ears and are desiring to hear something that sounds pleasing to the flesh that will not bother their sin. Regrettably, the nation and the world are full of such sermons, but let us say it again: There is no answer to the sin problem, no answer to the life and living problem, and no answer to the victory problem other than the Cross of Christ. We must ever understand that Christ is the source of all things that we receive from God, and the Cross is the means by which these things are given to us. It is all superintended by the Holy Spirit (Rom. 6:1-14; 8:1-11; I Cor. 1:17-18, 21, 23; 2:2; Gal., Chpt. 5; 6:14; Eph. 2:13-18; Col. 2:10-15). These Scriptures I've just given are only a tiny fraction of the Word of God that actually deals with this very subject.

It is the Cross! The Cross! The Cross!

DOMINION

Concerning David's victories, the Scripture says: *"And David smote Hadarezer king of Zobah unto Hamath, as he went to stablish his dominion by the river Euphrates."*

The upshot of this statement is that we either establish dominion over Satan and his powers of darkness, or he establishes dominion over us. As mentioned previously, the very name *Hadarezer* means "my demon helper."

As we've already stated, before David could defeat the enemy without, he had to first of all defeat the enemy within, which was the Philistines. I think I can say without fear of exaggeration that every single modern believer falls into the category of dominating Satan or being dominated by Satan. There is no in-between. There is only one way that the believer can establish dominion over the powers of darkness in whatever capacity they may come against us, and that is by the Cross of Christ. Whatever else the believer attempts to do—no matter how religious it might be and no matter how right it might be in its own way and manner—those things, whatever they might be, cannot be used to overcome the powers of darkness.

FALSE DIRECTIONS

Let me explain further. I heard a preacher over television the other day stating that if believers would take the Lord's Supper every day, or some such time frame, this would defeat all enemies, guarantee health and prosperity, etc. There is nothing like that in the Bible. While the Lord's Supper is most definitely scriptural, still, to try to use it in the wrong way will not bring about the desired results. If that were the case, Jesus needlessly came down here and died on a Cross.

I heard another preacher say that if a believer was experiencing bondage of any kind, he should establish a time that he would pray so much each day and read so many chapters in the Bible. Now, in fact, the believer's prayer life and Bible study are two of the most important things in one's life. Without a proper prayer life, one simply cannot have a proper relationship with the Lord. If one doesn't know the Word, then one is drifting without any direction. However, at the same time, as helpful as it may be in other means and ways, the idea that doing such will rid one of bondage is not biblical. Again, if one could overcome powers of darkness by praying so much each day and reading so many chapters, as important as that is, then Jesus didn't need to come down here and die on a Cross.

THE CROSS OF CHRIST

While all of these things we have named are very, very important, when we try to use them to establish dominion over the powers of darkness, we turn them into law, which God can never honor. Paul said it well:

"I do not frustrate the grace of God (if we make anything other than the Cross of Christ the object of our faith, we frustrate the grace of God, which means we stop its action, and the Holy Spirit will no longer help us)*: for if righteousness come by the law* (any type of law), *then Christ is dead in vain.* (If I can successfully live for the Lord by any means other than faith in Christ and the Cross, then the death of Christ was a waste.)*"* (Gal. 2:21) (The Expositor's Study Bible).

FRUSTRATING THE GRACE OF GOD

When the believer places his or her faith in anything (no matter how good it might be) other than Christ and the Cross, this frustrates the grace of God, which means that the good things the Lord desires to do for us are halted.

The *"grace of God"* is simply the goodness of God extended to undeserving saints. The truth is, God has no more grace today than He did under law. The difference is, due to the fact that animal blood was insufficient to remove sin, this hindered God from extending His goodness as He desired to the saints of that time.

Now, since the Cross, where every debt was paid and every sin cleansed, at least for all who will believe, God can pour grace upon any individual who will dare to believe Him. However, the trouble is, most of the modern church is frustrating the grace of God, and doing so by placing their faith in something other than the Cross of Christ.

THE APOSTLE PAUL

In connection with the statement as it regards frustrating the grace of God, the great apostle said:

I am crucified with Christ (as the foundation of all victory; Paul, here, takes us back to Romans 6:3-5): *nevertheless I live* (have new life); *yet not I* (not by my own strength and ability), *but Christ lives in me* (by virtue of me dying with Him on the Cross and being raised with Him in newness of life): *and the life which I now live in the flesh* (my daily walk before God) *I live by the faith of the Son of God* (the Cross is ever the object of my faith), *who loved me, and gave*

Himself for me (which is the only way that I could be saved) (Gal. 2:20) (The Expositor's Study Bible).

Two times in this one verse, Paul takes us straight to the Cross. This tells us that the Cross alone gives us victory. What Jesus there did, which was to offer Himself as a perfect sacrifice, satisfied the demands of a thrice-holy God. This refers to our faith in that finished work, and on an unending basis. Let us say it again:

CHRIST THE SOURCE

Christ is the source of all things that we receive from God, and the Cross is the means by which these things are done. It is all superintended by the Holy Spirit (Eph. 2:13-18).

All of this means that the believer can have dominion over the powers of darkness only by exercising faith in Christ and the Cross and, as stated, doing such on an unending, even daily, basis (Lk. 9:23). If the believer tries to live for God by any other manner, failure will be the guaranteed result.

IT IS FINISHED

The following article, "It Is Finished," was written some years ago by the late Oswald Chambers. It is a truth that needs to be read most carefully:

'I have finished the work which You gave me to do' (Jn. 17:4). The death of Jesus Christ is the performance in history of

the very mind of God. There is no room for looking on Jesus Christ as a martyr; His death was not something that happened to Him which might have been prevented: His death was the very reason why He came.

Never build your preaching of forgiveness on the fact that God is our Father, and He will forgive us because He loves us. It is untrue to Jesus Christ's revelation of God; it makes the Cross unnecessary, and the redemption 'much ado about nothing.' If God does forgive sin, it is because of the death of Christ. God could forgive men in no other way than by the death of His Son, and Jesus is exalted to be Savior because of His death. 'We see Jesus because of the suffering of death, crowned with glory and honor.' The greatest note of triumph that ever sounded in the ears of a startled universe was that sounded on the Cross of Christ – *it is finished.*' That is the last word in the redemption of man.

Anything that belittles or obliterates the holiness of God by a false view of the love of God, is untrue to the revelation of God given by Jesus Christ. Never allow the thought that Jesus Christ stands with us against God out of pity and compassion; that He became a curse for us out of sympathy with us. Jesus Christ became a curse for us by the divine decree. Our portion of realizing the terrific meaning of the curse is conviction of sin, the guilt of shame and penitence is given us; this is the great mercy of God. Jesus Christ hates the wrong in man, and Calvary is the estimate of His hatred.

PILLARS IN THE TEMPLE OF GOD

In defeating the enemies of Israel, which included various countries, the Scripture says that David *"took the shields of gold ... "* and, as well, *"... very much brass, wherewith Solomon made the brazen sea, and the pillars, and the vessels of brass."*

In addressing the church in Philadelphia, Jesus said, *"Him who overcomes will I make a pillar in the temple of My God"* (Rev. 3:12).

When He said this, He, no doubt, had in mind the two pillars that graced the front of the temple built by Solomon. Incidentally, this is the only building on planet Earth that was designed by God, and done so in totality. In fact, God was to reside between the mercy seat, the cherubim, and the Holy of Holies in the temple, which He did for several centuries.

The two pillars in front of the temple did not function as pillars normally do. In fact, the two pillars in front of the temple did not hold up anything. In other words, there was no porch or portico in front of the temple. The two pillars made of brass were strictly for ornamentation. In fact, one was named Jachin, which means "he shall establish," and the second was named Boaz, which means "in it is strength."

THE BELIEVER

The two pillars were 52.5 feet high, each with a 7.5–foot–tall chapter on top of each pillar, making each pillar a total of 60 feet tall.

There were chains at the tops of the pillars, which typified our union with Christ. Also, there were pomegranates carved into the brass, typifying the fruit of the Spirit.

The pillars faced the east, actually, the rising of the sun.

It is said that in coming to Jerusalem, travelers would at times camp out at night on Mount Olivet so they could watch the sun come up over the mountain. When it did each morning, with its rays striking the pillars, the burnished brass would throw off reflections of light that, it is said, was a sight to behold. Jesus, in essence, said that these pillars typified the child of God. This means that we aren't really needed in the great plan of God; therefore, one might as well refer to all believers as ornamentation. We must always remember that the beautiful reflection that comes from the Son is that of His light and not ours. We are only, as stated, a reflection of that light.

DAVID

Now when Tou king of Hamath heard how David had smitten all the host of Hadarezer king of Zobah; He sent Hadoram his son to king David, to inquire of his welfare, and to congratulate him, because he had fought against Hadarezer, and smitten him; (for Hadarezer had war with Tou;) and with him all manner of vessels of gold and silver and brass. Them also King David dedicated unto the LORD, with the silver and the gold that he brought from all these nations; from Edom, and from Moab, and from the children of Ammon, and from the Philistines, and from Amalek. Moreover Abishai the son of Zeruiah killed of the Edomites in the valley of salt eighteen thousand. And he put garrisons in Edom; and all the Edomites became David's servants. Thus the LORD *preserved David whithersoever he went. So David reigned over all Israel, and executed judgment and justice among all his people. And Joab the son of Zeruiah was over the host; and Jehoshaphat the son of Ahilud, recorder. And Zadok the son of Ahitub, and Abimelech the son of Abiathar, were the priests; and Shavsha was scribe; And Benaiah the son of Jehoiada was over the Cherethites and the Pelethites; and the sons of David were chief about the king* (I Chron. 18:9-17).

DEDICATED TO THE LORD

If the Lord does see fit to bless us with worldly riches, it must, without fail, be *"dedicated unto the* LORD*"* and not to our own selfish desires. Those who were with David experienced David's anointing.

Verse 13 is repeated from verse 6, and with purpose. It is meant to impress upon all that the Lord was the source of David's victories, and the Lord alone.

Verse 14 means that no enemy occupied any part of the land of Israel. How many of us can say that we reign over all the possession that God has given us? It can be done only through faith expressed in Christ and what Christ has done for us at the Cross, which then gives us the help of the Holy Spirit, without whom, nothing can be done (Rom. 8:1-2, 11).

The last two groups listed in verse 17 were probably Philistines who served as David's bodyguards. They had, thereby, thrown in their lot with David, consequently, forsaking their past, in effect, symbolic of all believers.

THE PRESERVATION OF THE LORD

The Scripture says, *"Thus the LORD preserved David whithersoever he went."*

When one is in the will of God, as obviously David was at this time, the Lord works for such a person, even as He worked for David. As a result, David won every conflict in which he was engaged. Besides that, he took into the coffers of Israel *"all manner of vessels of gold and silver and brass."* The Lord was with Israel, and as such, the nation would quickly rise to ascendancy. Every enemy would be defeated. Every power of darkness would be put down. The nation was now on the march.

Concerning this succession of victories, George Williams says: "The affection of David's heart for the people and house of God is evidenced by his consecrating the entire spoil of these victories to Jehovah's treasury. He kept nothing for himself. It shows rich spiritual experience on the part of Christian people when all the glory and profit of spiritual victories are denied to self, and willingly given to the enrichment of others, whether physically or spiritually."

O worship the King, all-glorious above;
O gratefully sing His power and His love:
Our Shield and Defender, the Ancient of Days,
Pavilioned in splendor and girded with praise.

O, tell of His might, O sing of His grace,
Whose robe is the light, Whose canopy space;
His chariots of wrath the deep thunderclouds form,
And dark is His path on the wings of the storm.

The earth, with its store of wonders untold,
Almighty, Your power has founded of old;
Has 'stablished it fast, by a changeless decree,
And round it has cast, like a mantle, the sea.

Your bountiful care, what tongue can recite?
It breathes in the air, it shines in the light;
It streams from the hills, it descends to the plain,
And sweetly distills in the dew and the rain.

Frail children of dust, and feeble as frail,
In You do we trust, nor find You to fail;
Your mercies, how tender, how firm to the end,
Our Maker, Defender, Redeemer, and Friend.

CHAPTER 3

THE SITE
SELECTED

THE SITE SELECTED

"THEN DAVID SAID, This is the house of the Lord *God, and this is the altar of the burnt offering for Israel. And David commanded to gather together the strangers that were in the land of Israel; and he set masons to hew wrought stones to build the house of God. And David prepared iron in abundance for the nails for the doors of the gates, and for the joinings; and brass in abundance without weight; Also cedar trees in abundance: for the Zidonians and they of Tyre brought much cedar wood to David. And David said, Solomon my son is young and tender, and the house that is to be built for the* Lord *must be exceeding magnificent, of fame and of glory throughout all countries: I will therefore now make preparation for it. So David prepared abundantly before his death"* (I Chron. 22:1-5).

The site had now been selected for where the temple would be built. It was all done totally by the Lord and none at all by the hand of man.

The *"strangers"* mentioned in verse 2 pertained to Gentiles who were craftsmen and, thereby, could provide skills not available among the Israelites.

In verse 3, we had the beginning of gathering the materials for the temple—not counted in the seven and a half years of the actual construction by Solomon.

This *"house"* was to be *in type* the millennial glory of the Messiah, just as the tabernacle had set forth His mediatorial glory.

THE HOUSE OF THE LORD

This one verse of Scripture (I Chron. 22:1), among other similar Scriptures, is the cause of much conflict in the Middle East, and more particularly, in Jerusalem. This is the site where Solomon, David's son, did build the great temple. As would be obvious, it is the most holy site in Judaism. As of now, the Muslim world controls this site, and yet, in the very near future, Israel will rebuild her temple on this very spot (Dan. 9:27).

Some have claimed that prophecy would be fulfilled even if the temple were built on another site or even next door to the Dome of the Rock; however, that is highly unlikely. Every indication is that when the temple is rebuilt in the future, even though nearly 2,000 years after Herod's temple occupied this site, it must be built on the same site that Solomon originally built the temple, which was approximately 3,000 years ago.

As stated, at the present, it is controlled by the Muslims. As well, they have no intention whatsoever of giving up this site, claiming it as the third most holy site in the world of Islam.

Islam claims that Ishmael was the promised seed instead of Isaac. They believe in God; however, it is a god of their own making. They claim that Muhammad was God's prophet. They also believe and teach that Jesus Christ was a great prophet but not equal to Muhammad, and certainly not the Son of God. They believe the only way to God is through Muhammad. Christianity and the Bible teach that the only way to God is through Jesus Christ (Jn. 14:6).

BIBLE PROPHECY

All of this means that for Bible prophecy to be fulfilled, the Dome of the Rock will have to be moved in order for the new Jewish temple to be built. How it will be done, especially at this time, no one knows, but it will be done. Once again, sacrifices will be offered up on the great altar, which will, as well, be placed in front of the temple just as it was with Solomon some 3,000 years ago. However, at the midpoint of the great tribulation, the Antichrist, who will enable Israel to rebuild her temple, will show his true colors and actually invade Israel. At that time, Israel will be defeated for the first time since becoming a nation in 1948. Were it not for the intervention of the Lord, she would be totally destroyed at this time; however, she will be preserved.

The Antichrist will take over the temple and make it his religious headquarters and will, thereby, stop the sacrifices. For all of this to happen, even as the Prophet Daniel proclaimed, the temple will have to be rebuilt, as would be obvious (Dan. 9:27).

One thing is certain: Whatever the Bible says will happen, that is exactly what will happen. The Bible is the Word of God, and when we speak of the Bible, we are speaking of a word-for-word translation, such as the King James. Unfortunately, there are untold numbers of religious books that go under the name of Bible, but which actually aren't. They are just merely a collection of religious thoughts and should in no fashion be looked at as the Word of God. As an example, I speak of those such as the *Message Bible.*

A POSSIBLE WAY

As we have briefly alluded, the Antichrist, who will soon arise on the world's scene, will be able to broker a peace treaty between Israel and the Muslims.

Thus, he will do that which the brightest minds in America have never been able to accomplish. The moment the seven-year agreement is signed, that is the moment the great tribulation begins.

Israel will accept this man as their Messiah. They will tell the whole world that this is the one. They will exclaim again and again that Jesus Christ was an imposter, etc. Many in the world, if not most, will accept what they say and herald the man, who has been able to broker a peace accord that no one else could, as the man of the hour. He will guarantee the borders of Israel, their protection, and their prosperity. He will even give them the right to rebuild their temple. Now, how will this be done?

What I'm about to say is in no way meant to claim that the Lord has shown me this, but I venture this scenario as a way in which it could possibly happen.

Before the great peace treaty is signed, the man of sin could call all of the Muslim leaders together. He could claim to be on their side, even though he hates every pretense of God in the world and will soon claim himself to be god.

At any rate, he could tell them that if they will go along with him, when the time is right, he will attack Israel, defeat her, give the entire country to the Muslims, and do everything possible to annihilate every Jew. His proposal would even include tearing down the Dome of the Rock and giving Israel permission to rebuild their temple on this spot. The Muslims will swallow hard on that demand.

With that being the case, one could see how they would readily agree to his proposal. Sure enough, at the midpoint of the great tribulation, he will attack Israel, meaning that she will suffer her first military defeat since becoming a nation in 1948. In fact, she would then be annihilated but for the intervention of the Lord. The man of sin will hear tidings (evil tidings) *"out of the east and out of the north"* (Dan. 11:44). He will break off from the destruction of Israel to go tend to these affairs, leaving Israel until the time of the battle of Armageddon. Israel will then realize that this man they had heralded as their Messiah was and is the very opposite. The Antichrist will take over the newly built temple, declare himself to be God, and will, in effect, declare war on all the religions in the world. In fact, he will herald his own person as the God of the ages (Dan. 11:37-39).

However, the Scripture says, *"Yet he shall come to his end, and none shall help him"* (Dan. 11:45). In other words, at the second coming, the Antichrist is going to find out just exactly who Jesus Christ really is, which will not be to his liking.

PREPARATION

As it regards the temple, the Scripture says, *"And David prepared."*

The preparation that David made as it regarded the temple, which was a monumental undertaking, was almost as detailed as the actual building of the structure.

In some way, any and every great work of God must be preceded by proper preparation. As well, even as the great work, whatever it might be, is prepared by the Holy Spirit, and the Holy Spirit alone, likewise, the Holy Spirit will conduct the preparation, but it will be by using men and women as instruments.

I was reading the other day the remarks of one particular preacher as it regarded David in his later years. He made the statement that because of the sin of David with Bath-sheba and the murder of her husband Uriah, which were dastardly sins indeed, in these later years (so said the preacher), David accomplished little for the Lord. The truth is, David probably accomplished more for the Lord after this terrible incident than before. Yes, he suffered much as well!

He wrote some 15 of the psalms after this terrible incident and probably more that are not accredited to him but, nevertheless, are the Word of God.

The psalms he wrote after this time are the following: 3, 4, 32, 38, 40, 41, 42, 43, 51, 55, 69, 72, 86, 109, 140.

As well, the preparation for the temple was without a doubt one of the most important works in which any individual could engage himself. We must quickly add that the Lord chose David to accomplish this most important task.

The temple was actually the place where God would dwell, in fact, the only place on earth where God would dwell. For the Lord to choose a person, even as He did David, to gather the materials with which the temple would be built was monumental indeed.

THE SWEET SINGER OF ISRAEL

None of my statements are meant to minimize the effect of the terrible sin committed by David. To be sure, David paid dearly for that which he did; however, it did not stop the Lord from using him, and it was because David promptly repented of this foul deed.

Whether they realize it or not, preachers, or anyone for that matter, who suggest that a person cannot be used because of failure in the past have just eliminated the entirety of the body of Christ.

In other words, God wouldn't be able to use anyone. Anyone who doesn't know that fact does not know the Bible as he should, does not know himself as he should, and above all, doesn't know the Lord as he should. It all comes under justification by faith.

A LACK OF REPENTANCE AND UNBELIEF

The only thing that disqualifies a person from being used of the Lord is lack of repentance and unbelief. When the Lord forgives a person, even as He forgave David and has forgiven every one of us, we are forgiven totally and completely. In other words, justification demands that in the mind of God, the terrible sin, whatever it may be, no longer even exists. The Lord has no black marks beside the name of any believer. We should understand that! When we, as believers, are forgiven and cleansed, the action is blotted out as if it never existed. What a wonderful Lord we serve!

However, again I state that this in no way is meant to minimize sin. Because the Lord will forgive and cleanse doesn't mean there isn't payment. Sin is so awful, so bad, so destructive, and so degrading that it must never be looked at with any degree of impunity. It is so bad, in fact, that it took the Cross with all of its implications to eliminate this mad monster. In fact, all sin is a form of insanity.

However, thank God that there was and is a Cross. There the matter was settled and settled forever. Satan is a master at telling believers that if they have done something wrong, even though they have properly repented, they are on God's blacklist. Don't believe it. The sad fact is that Satan uses preachers to peddle his lies. Irrespective, you must not believe it.

WHAT TYPE OF PREPARATION?

I'm sure the *type* of preparation would be as different as the individuals involved. Considering that with something so delicate, the Lord allowed David to use his own personal experience, I will use mine as well.

In 1991, the ministry was in shambles. I did not know what to do, but I did know that the fault was mine, but yet, I didn't know quite how it was mine. Despite the pain and suffering, this was the beginning of the preparation of the great revelation of the Cross that the Lord ultimately would give me. At that time, almost the entirety of the church world was screaming, and screaming loudly, that I not preach anymore. I must stop all ministry, etc.

I did have the presence of mind to know and understand that at this time, especially at this time, I must have the leading of the Lord. If I missed it here, I would be destroyed forever.

At the very heart of sorrow and heartache—a pain so unimaginable that it defies description—eight or 10 of us gathered for prayer one night. If I remember it correctly, it was a Thursday night in October 1991. In that prayer session, the Holy Spirit came down in such a way that I have seldom seen or witnessed. There was a word of prophecy given, and this is what it was:

I AM NOT A MAN THAT I SHOULD LIE

"I'm not a man that I should lie, neither the son of man that I should repent. What I have blessed, nothing can curse!"

I had my answer, and in unmistakable terms. The Lord had called me to preach when I was but a child. He had not lied about it, neither had He changed His mind, and never will He change His mind. It didn't matter what man said, I was to do what He said that I had to do. Thank God for that moving of the

Spirit on that Thursday night in October 1991. As well, thank God that I had the presence of the Holy Spirit to know exactly what the Lord was saying. As stated, it was the beginning of the preparation time.

The next morning, if I remember correctly, on my way to the office, the Lord spoke to my heart and told me to begin two prayer meetings a day, morning and night.

The very first prayer meeting we conducted was at the office. There must have been about 15 or 20 at that particular meeting, and the Spirit of God, once again, moved in a mighty, mighty way.

I knew the Lord had told me to continue preaching, but I wondered if that meant I was to stay on television or not! There is no greater medium for reaching people with the Gospel than television, and even though in the aggregate, it is probably the least expensive of presentations, still, it costs a lot of money to make and air the programming. Untold numbers of people are reached, but it costs much money to do it. That morning, as I began to importune the Lord as to what I should do as it regarded television, once again, the Lord spoke to my heart. He said:

"I have called you for media ministry, and I have not lifted that call."

My next thought was, How can we pay for the telecast?

THE ANSWER OF THE LORD

In answer to my question, the Lord took me to Matthew, Chapter 17. The incident there recorded is found only in Matthew, but it answered my question readily.

The tax collector came to Peter, in effect, stating that taxes were owed. Peter went to the Lord and asked Him if, in fact, the taxes were owed. In essence, Jesus said, *"No,"* but then stated, *"Notwithstanding, lest we should offend them, you go to the sea, and cast an hook, and take up the fish that first comes up; and when you have opened his mouth, you shall find a piece of money: that take, and give unto them from Me and you"* (Mat. 17:27).

The Lord then spoke to my heart, saying, "In the manner that I met the need that day regarding the taxes, in like manner I will meet the need of the telecast and the ministry as a whole."

I knew it was the Lord who had spoken to me. His presence was undeniable; however, I also knew this was the most unorthodox manner of raising funds that anyone has ever known.

How unorthodox—catching a fish, looking in its mouth, finding a piece of money (a coin), and with that paying the taxes.

However, that's exactly the way the Lord has provided for this ministry. He has performed miracle after miracle in order that the finances be met, many times from totally unexpected sources.

There have been countless times in the last nearly 20 years that I didn't see how we could make it, but every time, sometimes at the last moment, the Lord would always come through.

As should be obvious, in all of this, He was and is teaching me trust. It all had to do, and has to do, with the preparation.

THE REVELATION

Then, in 1997, the Lord opened up to me truths from His Word that I had not previously known, which would revolutionize my life and ministry. To be sure, it was not new but that which had actually been given to the Apostle Paul. Also, to be sure, we kept up those prayer meetings twice a day, with the exception of service times, for all of those years. In fact, I personally still continue that agenda of prayer.

First of all, the Lord showed me why Christians fail, despite trying so very hard not to fail. He took me to Chapter 6 of Romans and there explained the sin nature to me. However, even though the revelation He gave me was of such magnitude as to be beyond compare, still, that morning, He didn't tell me the solution to the problem of the sin nature. That would come several days later.

(The Lord used the book on Romans authored by Kenneth Wuest, the Baptist theologian, to help me understand the sin nature.)

In prayer meeting a week or so later, the Lord again moved upon my heart greatly and told me the following as it concerned the answer to the sin nature. It came in three short sentences:

1. "The answer for which you seek is found in the Cross."

2. "The solution for which you seek is found in the Cross."

3. "The answer for which you seek is found *only* in the Cross."

Once again the Lord took me to the great sixth chapter of Romans.

THE HOLY SPIRIT

If the answer is found solely in the Cross, which is what the Lord told me, where does that leave the Holy Spirit? That question came immediately to my mind that morning.

I knew beyond the shadow of a doubt that the Holy Spirit plays a tremendous part in all that is done as it regards the work of God on earth. However, I was left that day not really knowing or understanding just how He works as it regards the Cross and its involvement in our lives.

A few weeks later, the Lord gave me the answer to that by taking me to Romans 8:2, which says: *"For the law of the Spirit of life in Christ Jesus has made me free from the law of sin and death."*

I knew then how the Holy Spirit works. He works entirely within the framework of the finished work of Christ. In other words, it is the Cross that gives the Holy Spirit the legal means to do all that He does in our hearts and lives. It is the Cross of Christ that has made it all possible. Please look at the simple diagram:

- Jesus Christ is the source of all things we receive from God (Jn. 1:1, 14, 29; 14:6).

- The Cross of Christ is the means that makes all these things possible (Rom. 6:1-14; Col. 2:10-15).

- This means that Christ and what He did for us at the Cross must always and without exception be the object of our faith (I Cor. 1:17-18, 23; 2:2).

- With Christ as our source, the Cross of Christ as the means, and our faith anchored squarely in Christ and the Cross, the Holy Spirit—who works exclusively within the parameters of the finished work of Christ—can then work mightily on our behalf (Rom. 8:1-11; Eph. 2:13-18).

To be sure, I'm only touching the high spots of this revelation, as I've already stated some pages back, and I would strongly recommend that the reader secure for himself a copy of the book entitled, *The Message of the Cross.* This particular book will go into much greater detail, and I feel will be a great blessing to you.

THE REVELATION OF THE CROSS

I was to find out that this revelation given to me was of far greater degree than I could ever begin to imagine. In fact, I believe that it is a word from the Lord for the entirety of the church world at this hour. I believe this is what the Holy Spirit is presently saying to the churches.

During these some six years of conducting two prayer meetings a day, the Lord never really told me why He directed me to do this—with one exception. He said to me at the outset, "Do not seek Me so much for what I can do, but rather for who I am."

In other words, He was speaking of relationship. It took much preparation for that revelation to be given, and to be frank, the preparation has not ceased from then until now. I suspect that it will never cease.

DAVID AND SOLOMON

Then he called for Solomon his son, and charged him to build an house for the LORD God of Israel. And David said to Solomon, My son, as for me, it was in my mind to build an house unto the name of the LORD my God: But the Word of the LORD came to me saying, You have shed blood abundantly, and have made great wars: you shall not build an house unto My name, because you have shed much blood upon the earth in My sight. Behold, a son shall be born to you, who shall be a man of rest; and I will give him rest from all his enemies round about: for his name shall be Solomon, and I will give peace and quietness unto Israel in his days. He shall build an house for My name; and he shall be My son, and I will be his father; and I will establish the throne of his kingdom over Israel forever. Now, my son, the LORD be with you; and prosper you, and build the house of the Lord your God, as He has said of you. Only the LORD give you wisdom and understanding, and give you charge concerning Israel, that you may keep the law of the LORD your God. Then shall you prosper, if you take heed to fulfill the statutes and judgments which the LORD charged Moses with concerning Israel: be strong, and of good courage; dread not, nor be dismayed. Now, behold, in my trouble I have prepared for the house of the LORD an hundred thousand talents of gold, and a thousand thousand talents of silver; and of brass and iron without weight; for it is in abundance: timber also and stone have I prepared; and you may add thereto. Moreover there are workmen with you in abundance, hewers and workers of stone and timber, and all manner of cunning men for every manner of work. Of the gold, the silver, and the brass, and the iron, there is no number. Arise therefore, and be doing, and the LORD be with you. David also commanded all the princes of Israel to help Solomon his son, saying, Is not the LORD your God with you? and has He not given you rest on every side? for He has given the inhabitants of the land into my hand; and the land is subdued before the LORD, and before His people. Now set your heart and your soul to seek the LORD your God; arise therefore, and build you the sanctuary of the LORD God, to bring the ark of the covenant of the LORD, and the holy vessels of God, into the house that is to be built to the name of the LORD (I Chron. 22:6-19).

THE PRINCE OF PEACE

According to verse 6, Solomon was chosen by the Lord (I Kings 1:30, 37, 39). David typifies Christ as a Man of War destroying His enemies; Solomon typifies Christ as the Prince of Peace reigning over a kingdom free from these enemies. Verse 9 proclaims that Solomon was named before he was born. He was one of seven men in the Bible named before birth.

The complete fulfillment of verse 10 will be in Christ and will take place in the coming kingdom age (Isa., Chpt. 11).

The words spoken in verse 12 may have been the germ of Solomon's own prayer, which *"pleased the LORD"* (I Kings 3:5-14; II Chron. 1:7-12).

Basically, in verse 13, David quotes the very words given by the Lord to Joshua, which were given about 500 years earlier; however, a general promise given by the Lord is applicable to anyone who will dare to believe.

The 100,000 talents of gold of verse 14 would be worth approximately $150 billion or more in 2017 currency.

All that David said in his admonishment to Solomon confirmed what so often appears in the character of this man—that all through his stormy life of warfare, his heart was true to one great purpose, the establishment of the house of God and the peace of God in the midst of the people of God.

At long last, every enemy had been defeated, and the great promises of God were being brought to fulfillment.

DAVID AND SOLOMON, BOTH TYPES OF CHRIST

David was a type of Christ as it regarded the mediatorial glory of our Lord. Solomon was a type of Christ as it regarded the millennial glory of the Messiah. Regarding the mediation of Christ, many enemies had to be defeated, which were defeated at the Cross. The millennial glory is yet to come and will proclaim a time when all enemies are defeated, a time of peace and prosperity such as the world has never known before. As stated, David typified the former, while his son Solomon typified the latter.

Concerning this, George Williams says: "David typifies Christ as a man of war destroying his enemies, and Solomon, as Christ the Prince of Peace, reigning over a Kingdom made free from these enemies."

And yet, all types are imperfect, as should be overly obvious. Consequently, many might ask the question of how David could be a type of Christ, especially considering the terrible sins he committed. Others may point to Solomon and ask the same question, especially considering that he lost his way in his older years but, hopefully, came back at the end.

JUSTIFICATION BY FAITH

Once again, justification by faith is the answer and, in fact, the only answer.

There are no perfect human beings. In fact, there has never been a perfect human being, with one exception, and that is our Lord and Saviour, Jesus Christ. He alone was perfect, pure, and without corruption of any nature. Therefore, when the believing sinner says "yes" to Christ, the sin of the sinner is loaded onto the Saviour, while the perfection of the Redeemer is given freely to the believing sinner. Two of the sacrifices of old typified this perfectly.

In the sin offering, the sin of the individual, whatever it may have been, was loaded on Christ. The whole burnt offering represented the very opposite. It presented the totality of the perfection of Christ given to the sinner. Even as I dictate these notes, I sense the presence of God. My sins are no more because they've all been given to Him, and He atoned for them on the Cross. On top of that, He has given me His glorious perfection. What a mighty God we serve!

David typified redemption, while Solomon typified peace.

PROSPERITY

Pure and simple, the Holy Spirit through David told his son, *"The* LORD *be with you; and prosper you, and build the house of the* LORD *your God, as He has said of you. Only the* LORD *give you wisdom and understanding, and give you charge concerning Israel, that you may keep the law of the* LORD *your God. Then shall you prosper, if you take heed to fulfill the statutes and judgments which the* LORD *charged Moses with concerning Israel: be strong, and of a good courage; dread not, nor be dismayed."* (I Chronicles 22:11-13).

Several things were demanded of Solomon. They were:

- Solomon was not to fail in the building of the house of the Lord.

- He was to keep the law of the Lord his God.

- He was to take heed to fulfill the statutes and judgments with which the Lord charged Moses concerning Israel.

- He was to be strong and of a good courage. As well, he was not to fear or be dismayed.

I don't think there is much difference in these commands than those given to us presently.

But yet, given the weakness of humanity in even the best of believers, how can these commandments be kept?

Paul addressed this over and over again. In fact, most of his teachings centered on this very question: How can the believer live an overcoming, victorious life, victorious over the world, the flesh, and the Devil? It was to Paul that the meaning of the new covenant was given, and actually, that meaning is the Cross.

THE APOSTLE PAUL

Paul could be quoted in many capacities regarding this but please notice the following:

> And if Christ be in you (He is in you through the power and person of the Spirit [Gal. 2:20]), the body is dead because of sin (means that the physical body has been rendered helpless because of the fall; consequently, the believer trying to overcome by willpower presents a fruitless task); but the Spirit is life because of righteousness (only the Holy Spirit can make us what we ought to be, which means we cannot do it ourselves; once again, He performs all that He does within the parameters, so to speak, of the finished work of Christ) (Rom. 8:10) (The Expositor's Study Bible).

The phrase, "The body is dead because of sin," proclaims the fact that we are physically unable to do what is demanded of us.

It may seem so simple, but the sad fact is, the believer cannot keep the commandments of the Lord by his own strength, ability, power, education, intellect, motivation, etc. So, how are the commandments to be kept?

HOW THE COMMANDMENTS ARE KEPT

Jesus Christ as our substitute, whom Paul referred to as the *"last Adam"* and the *"second Man,"* has already kept all the commandments on our behalf. He lived a perfect life, never failing even one time in word, thought, or deed. Then, as He kept the law of God, and did so perfectly in His life and living, He addressed the broken law by going to the Cross and giving Himself in sacrifice. The thing is, He did it all for us, and He did it for us simply because we could not do it ourselves.

That seems to be difficult for most believers to comprehend, to understand, or to accept. Once we are saved and Spirit-filled, we tend to think that we can do anything. In fact, one of the most oft quoted Scriptures is, *"I can do all things through Christ who strengthens me"* (Phil. 4:13).

While, of course, the Word of God is most certainly true, still, we must understand what Paul was talking about when he mentioned *"all things."*

ALL THINGS

It's not all things that we want, but rather all things that He wants and desires. He will never strengthen us to disobey Him, to circumvent His will, or to dishonor His Word, which should be obvious. He will only strengthen us to carry out His will, whatever that will might be.

The way and, in fact, the only way that the commandments of the Lord can be kept (this goes for all believers) is for the believer to understand that within himself, he cannot hope to please the Lord in doing what he must do. We fall short, in fact, woefully short!

It is the Holy Spirit alone who can carry out the will of God in our lives, develop His fruit, and help us to grow in grace and the knowledge of the Lord. The Holy Spirit alone can accomplish this.

And yet, we don't see Him carrying out all of these great things in the hearts and lives of most believers. Why?

THE HOLY SPIRIT

The Holy Spirit doesn't require very much of us. If He did, none of us would make it; however, He does require one thing and, in fact, demands it. That one thing is that our faith be exclusively in Christ and the Cross. We must understand the following:

- We must ever understand that Christ is the source of all things we receive from God.

- The Cross is the means by which these things are given to us.

- This means that Christ and the Cross are to ever be the object of our faith.

- With all of this being done, the Holy Spirit, who super-intends it all, will work mightily on our behalf. The Holy Spirit works exclusively within the parameters of the finished work of Christ (Rom. 6:1-14; 8:1-11; I Cor. 1:17-18, 21, 23; 2:2; Gal., Chpt. 5; 6:14; Eph. 2:13-18; Col. 2:10-15).

We must ever know and understand that the Cross of Christ plays just as much an abundant part in our lives and living as it did in our initial salvation experiences. We are to look to Christ and what Christ did at the Cross for everything. The Holy Spirit will not tolerate anything else. In other words, the Cross of Christ, as stated, must ever be the object of our faith.

With this being done, and maintained we might quickly add, the Holy Spirit, who works strictly within the parameters of the finished work of Christ, will then work mightily on our behalf and do what only He can do. The commandments will then be kept, in fact, without us even thinking about it.

BUILD THE HOUSE OF THE LORD

The command given to Solomon by David so long, long ago, as it regarded building the house of the Lord, is just as apropos presently as it was then. Of course, there is a great difference now but, in essence, the command is the same.

Then, it was a physical house, as is overly obvious. Now, it is a spiritual house.

This spiritual house referred to as the *new covenant* concerns our life and living in every respect. Concerning this, Paul said: *"Know you not that you are the temple of God* (where the Holy Spirit abides), *and that the Spirit of God dwells in you?* (That makes the born-again believer His permanent home.)*"* (I Cor. 3:16) (The Expositor's Study Bible).

Then, it was a corporate situation, while now, it is a personal affair.

The Spirit of God was to dwell between the mercy seat and the cherubim in the house that Solomon built. Due to the Cross where the price was paid, the Holy Spirit (just as we have quoted) now resides within our hearts and lives, and does so forever.

THE TEMPLE OF GOD

But yet, the Lord warns us by saying,

If any man defile the temple of God (our physical bodies must be a living sacrifice, which means that we stay holy by ever making the Cross the object of our faith [Rom. 12:1]), *him shall God destroy* (to fail to function in God's prescribed order [the Cross] opens the believer up to Satan, which will ultimately result in destruction); *for the temple of God is holy, which temple you are.* (We are 'holy' by virtue of being 'in Christ.' We remain holy by the work of the Holy Spirit, who demands that our faith ever be in the Cross, which has made all of this possible) (I Cor. 3:17) (The Expositor's Study Bible).

Israel of old ultimately defiled their temple, and even as the Prophet Ezekiel portrayed the fact, the Lord destroyed it. He had no alternative or choice!

The same is said for the temple of our body, which houses the Spirit of God. Please understand the following: To guarantee against destruction of this temple, our faith must ever be in the Cross of Christ. God will always honor that faith and, in fact, He will honor no other type of faith. This is the only manner in which our bodies, our life and living, etc., can be kept free, pure, and clean. It is faith in Christ, ever faith in Christ and what Christ has done for us at the Cross.

THE CROSS

Some have claimed that we make too much of the Cross! How can this be when we consider that the Cross of Christ is the greatest display of the wisdom of God ever given to us? It is even greater than His creation of the universe and even greater than His creation of man (I Cor. 2:6-8). How is it possible for one to make too much of the great plan of redemption? Please understand that the Cross is not just one of many steps as it regards redemption; it is the entirety of the plan of God. We must never forget that without the Cross, there could not have been a resurrection. Also, if Jesus had failed to atone for even one sin, He could not have been raised from the dead, considering that the wages of sin is death. However, the fact that He was raised from the dead proclaims to us that He atoned for all sin, past, present, and future, at least for all who will believe (Jn. 3:16).

That's the reason that every doctrine must be built squarely upon the foundation of the Cross of Christ. If it is built otherwise, every single time, it will fall out to false doctrine.

We are to continue to build the house, which means to grow in grace and the knowledge of the Lord. Every believer ought to be closer to the Lord today than they were yesterday. This spiritual growth can only be brought about by the believer ever understanding more and more about the Cross, which the Holy Spirit will bring to fruition in our lives if we will only walk a path of obedience respecting the great plan of God.

It is ever the Cross! The Cross! The Cross!

Give to our God immortal praise!
Mercy and truth are all His ways;
Wonders of grace to God belong,
Repeat His mercies in your song.

Give to the Lord of lords renown,
The King of kings with glory crown;
His mercies ever shall endure,
When lords and kings are known no more.

He saw the Gentiles dead in sin,
And felt His pity work within;
His mercies ever shall endure,
When death and sin shall reign no more.

He sent His Son with power to save,
From guilt, and darkness, and the grave,
Wonders of grace to God belong,
Repeat His mercies in your song.

CHAPTER 4

MUSIC

MUSIC

"MOREOVER DAVID AND THE captains of the host separated to the service of the sons of Asaph, and of Heman, and of Jeduthun, who should prophesy with harps, with psalteries, and with cymbals: and the number of the workmen according to their service was: Of the sons of Asaph; Zaccur, and Joseph, and Nethaniah, and Asarelah, the sons of Asaph under the hands of Asaph, which prophesied according to the order of the king. Of Jeduthun: the sons of Jeduthun; Gedaliah, and Zeri, and Jeshaiah, Hashabiah, and Mattithiah, six, under the hands of their father Jeduthun, who prophesied with a harp, to give thanks and to praise the LORD. Of Heman: the sons of Heman; Bukkiah, Mattaniah, Uzziel, Shebuel, and Jerimoth, Hananiah, Hanani, Eliathah, Giddalti, and Romamti-ezer, Joshbekashah, Mallothi, Hothir, and Mahazioth: All these were the sons of Heman the king's seer in the words of God, to lift up the horn. And God gave to Heman fourteen sons and three daughters. All these were under the hands of their father for song in the house of the LORD, with cymbals, psalteries, and harps, for the service of the house of God, according to the king's order to Asaph, Jeduthun, and Heman. So the number of them, with their brethren who were instructed in the songs of the

LORD, *even all who were cunning, was two hundred four score and eight. And they cast lots, ward against ward, as well the small as the great, the teacher as the scholar"* (I Chron. 25:1-8).

MUSICAL INSTRUMENTATION

We are now told of the division of the 4,000 singers into 24 courses or weekly periods.

There was no such provision for song and worship in the tabernacle in the wilderness as in the temple of Solomon. This was because the former spoke of a provided redemption, while the latter spoke of an accomplished salvation. According to this Word, musical instrumentation that accompanies Spirit-led singing is constituted as *"prophecy"* (I Cor. 14:3).

The overseership of this service of worship as it regarded music and singing seems to have been divided among the sons of Asaph, Jeduthun, and Heman.

These 4,000 singers would have been divided into 24 choirs, with a little bit over 250 members to the choir, except, no doubt, for special occasions when several of the choirs, or even all of the singers, would have joined together. Also, according to verse 7, these choirs were helped by the 288 skilled musicians and skilled singers.

MUSIC, SINGING, WORSHIP, AND PROPHECY

The reader should well note the volume of praise that was to fill the temple area and all of Jerusalem. It was symbolic of that which will fill not only the temple area in Jerusalem during the coming kingdom age but, as well, the entirety of the earth. The great Prophet Isaiah said: *"For the earth shall be full of the knowledge of the Lord, as the waters cover the sea"* (Isa. 11:9). As well, in our present day churches, volumes of praise should fill the sanctuary constantly. Inasmuch as we are now the temple of the Holy Spirit (I Cor. 3:16), a volume of praise to the Lord should fill our hearts constantly. Surely by now the Bible student has learned the premium that God places on praise. Jesus came from the tribe of Judah, and its tribal name means "praise."

THE OVERSEERSHIP

The overseership of this service seemed to be divided among the following:

- The sons of Asaph
- The sons of Jeduthun
- The sons of Heman

They were given charge of the great choirs and the musicians with a spiritual term being attached to such, *"who should prophesy with harps, with psalteries, and with cymbals."* The *"songs of the Lord"* were basically the same as that which would be given in I Corinthians 14:3, which speaks to men of edification, exhortation, and comfort. This was accomplished by the singing and the music and is, as well, accomplished thusly today.

In other words, when anyone sings *"the songs of the LORD,"* which will always glorify God, he is, in effect, prophesying. We would do well to note that the Holy Spirit is the One who used the word prophesy. For such to be, the *flesh* must have no place, but only the *Spirit.* Sadly, too much of that which passes for Christian music emphasizes the flesh instead of the Spirit.

MUSIC HAS THREE CHARACTERISTICS

1. Melody

2. Harmony

3. Rhythm

All three coordinate with each other to produce the worship that the Holy Spirit intends. So-called contemporary Christian music destroys the harmony and the melody; consequently, it neither produces nor elicits praise. Efforts to worship thusly are fruitless.

Likewise, rhythm is legitimate and scriptural, providing measures of accompaniment according to the cymbal, etc.—unless it is rhythm for the sake of rhythm, thereby, catering solely to the flesh. Then it becomes spiritually illegitimate.

As we read this particular chapter, we are actually reading the formation of music given by the Holy Spirit to David, which formed the foundation of all spiritual music from then until now. To show how important music and singing are as it regards worship, the Psalms, which are 150 songs, constitute the longest book in the Bible. The fact that the Holy Spirit delegated the longest book in the Bible to the worship provided by music and singing lets us know how important it actually is.

SONGS OF THE LORD

Concerning the singers and the musicians, the Scripture says, *"Who were instructed in the songs of the LORD."* What a beautiful statement! These *"songs of the LORD"* made up at this particular time at least part of the Psalms, as we now know them.

The Holy Spirit takes special note, as verse 4 says, of Heman and his 14 sons. In the Hebrew, it seems that the names of his sons form a sentence, and this sentence glorifies God—*lifting up the horn.* The Holy Spirit specifically says, *"And God gave to Heman fourteen sons and three daughters,"* meaning that these were especially used in the service of the Lord. How blessed Heman was!

These choirs were very lively in their worship, hence, the different types of percussion instrumentation used.

Tradition says that at times the choirs of Israel would be divided into two sections, with the men on one side and the ladies on the other. A phrase or a stanza would be sung by one group and then answered by the other. Thus, the temple was to be filled with songs. As well, praise will characterize the great kingdom age soon to come. So, today, an accomplished salvation fills the believer's mouth with singing and with praise.

Praise Him! Praise Him!
Jesus, our blessed Redeemer!
Sing, O earth, His wonderful love proclaim!
Hail Him! Hail Him!
Highest archangels in glory;
Strength and honor give to His holy name!
Like a shepherd Jesus will guard His children,
In His arms He carries them all day long.

Praise Him! Praise Him!
Jesus, our blessed Redeemer!
For our sins He suffered, and bled and died;
He our Rock, our hope of eternal salvation,
Hail Him! Hail Him!
Jesus the Crucified.
Sound His praises!
Jesus who bore our sorrows;
Love unbounded, wonderful,
Deep and strong.

Praise Him! Praise Him!
Jesus, our blessed Redeemer!
Heavenly portals loud with hosannas ring!
Jesus, Saviour reigneth forever and ever,
Crown Him! Crown Him!
Prophet and Priest and King!
Christ is coming! Over the world victorious,
Power and glory unto the Lord belong.

CHAPTER 5

THE KINGDOM

CHAPTER FIVE

THE KINGDOM

*"AND DAVID ASSEMBLED ALL the princes of Israel, the princes
of the tribes, and the captains of the companies who ministered to
the king by course, and the captains over the thousands, and captains over the hundreds, and the stewards over all the substance and
possession of the king, and of his sons, and with the officers, and
with the mighty men, and with all the valiant men, unto Jerusalem.
Then David the king stood up upon his feet, and said, Hear me, my
brethren, and my people: As for me, I had in my heart to build an
house of rest for the ark of the covenant of the LORD, and for the
footstool of our God, and had made ready for the building: But God
said unto me, You shall not build an house for My name, because you
have been a man of war, and have shed blood. Howbeit the LORD
God of Israel chose me before all the house of my father to be king
over Israel forever: for he has chosen Judah to be the ruler; and of
the house of Judah, the house of my father; and among the sons of
my father He liked me to make me king over all Israel: And of all
my sons, (for the LORD has given me many sons,) He has chosen
Solomon my son to sit upon the throne of the kingdom of the LORD
over Israel. And He said unto me, Solomon your son, he shall build*

My house and My courts: for I have chosen him to be My son, and I will be his father. Moreover I will establish his kingdom forever, if he be constant to do My commandments and My judgments, as at this day. Now therefore in the sight of all Israel the congregation of the LORD, and in the audience of our God, keep and seek for all the commandments of the LORD your God: that you may possess this good land, and leave it for an inheritance for your children after you forever" (I Chron. 28:1-8).

THE HOUSE OF GOD

In his dying hour, the address of David to his people was more concerned with the house of God than with anything else in his kingdom.

The expression found in verse 5, which is not found in its entirety elsewhere, is an emphatic statement of the true theocracy. This should have ever prevailed among the people of Israel but was set aside because of failure on the part of Israel. It is now paralleled by the kingship of our Lord in His own church.

For a time, Solomon was a child of God. He loved the Lord and walked in all His statutes (I Ki. 3:3), and the Lord loved him (II Sam. 12:24). However, in later life, Solomon grew cold toward Jehovah and loved many strange women, who turned his heart away from God (I Ki. 11:1-8). The Lord then became angry with Solomon and turned against him in his backslidings (I Ki. 11:9-40). The Lord then took his kingdom from him and finally destroyed it, all because of sin. The kingdom will be renewed again when Israel comes to repentance, which she will immediately after the second coming (Zech. 12:10). Under the Messiah, the true David, and, in fact, the true Solomon, this kingdom will continue eternally.

THE LAST ASSEMBLY

It must have taken several weeks, and possibly even several months, for the message to go out all over Israel concerning this assembly that David called. It would be his last one.

Israel was now at the height of power. Every enemy was defeated. Solomon, God's will as the titular leader of this great people, had already been enthroned.

The people of Israel constituted the only people on earth who had a knowledge of Jehovah. Every other nation in the world was polytheistic, meaning they worshipped many gods, in effect, demon spirits. Israel alone knew the Lord and knew His ways, which, in effect, placed them light years ahead of anyone else on earth.

And yet, they were not raised up to become an empire, but rather, their mission was threefold.

A THREEFOLD MISSION

1. They were to give the world the Word of God, which they did. All the writers of every book of the Bible were Jewish, with possibly the exception of Luke. However, it is my belief that Luke was Jewish as well.

2. They were to serve as the womb of the Messiah. The Lord, the Prince of Glory, would be born to these people. He was actually born of a virgin, which was a miracle of miracles within itself, and was all prophesied by Isaiah (Isa. 7:14). Tragically, when Christ was born, Israel did not recognize their Messiah and ultimately crucified Him. This problem will have to be rectified before certain things can be done, and it most certainly will at the second coming. Then Israel will see the terrible mistake they made—a mistake that caused them untold suffering and sorrow—and will then truly engage in repentance. They will then be able to carry out that which the Lord originally intended for them.

3. They were raised up to evangelize the world, meaning to show the world the one true God. In a sense, through the Apostle Paul and the original apostles, plus others from Israel, they did this. We have the Gospel today because of what these men did so long, long ago. Most in the early church of that time, and we speak of the leaders, died a martyr's death. It is believed that John the Beloved was the only one of the original apostles who died a natural death. In other words, they gave their all for the cause of Christ, and today we have the Gospel because of the price they paid.

So, even though Israel, and we speak of natural Israel, hated Christ and crucified Him, nevertheless, there were certain ones in Israel who did not hate Him. They came to be flaming lights for the spread of the Gospel that they began, which ultimately touched the entirety of this world.

The question must be asked, I suppose, as to how much delay was brought about by Israel's self-will and tremendous failures respecting her walk with the Lord.

That question, I think, is impossible to answer. Unfortunately, every single believer on the face of the earth, more or less, falls into the same category. How much do we hinder the Lord by our unbelief? How much do we miss the mark by going astray because of self-will? How much is the Lord hindered by these wild actions on our part?

Disobedience does definitely hinder, and hinder greatly; however, I think the Lord takes everything into consideration and works everything out accordingly, but according to His timetable.

THE TEMPLE OF THE LORD

As we have previously stated, as David came down to the end of his life's journey, his mind and heart were totally on that which the Lord had ordained that He do. Were there regrets?

There are always regrets; however, the regrets were behind, and David was now preparing for the construction of the temple to a degree that you and I cannot comprehend.

He had desperately wanted to build the temple himself; however, the Lord bluntly told him that he would not build the house, *"because you have been a man of war, and have shed blood."*

So, his son Solomon would build the temple, and it would be the grandest building on the face of the earth. It is the only building per se where the Lord actually dwelt. In fact, the great Prophet Ezekiel tells us in his writings exactly when the Lord left the temple (Ezek. 11:23). The great prophet also saw the Spirit of the Lord return, but that is yet future. It will be during the time of the coming kingdom age when Jesus Christ will rule personally from Jerusalem after the millennial temple is built (Ezek. 43:1-7). This means that the Lord did not actually dwell in Zerubbabel's temple, which was constructed after the dispersion, nor did the Lord dwell in Herod's temple.

JUDAH

The reason is clear. In both cases, Israel was no longer her own, but rather a vassal state ruled by another, and all because of sin.

In verse 4, David makes the statement, *"For He has chosen Judah to be the ruler."*

What did this mean?

Of course, David was speaking of the tribe of Judah, which was the largest of all the tribes. It was the tribe from which he came and from which our Lord would come, with the latter referring most of all to the meaning of the phrase. Everything centered around the Lord Jesus Christ, and we speak of the temple in its entirety, with all of its rituals and ceremonies. In some way, every part and parcel of the temple and every ceremony spoke of Christ in His atoning work, mediatorial work, or intercessory work. As well, the temple proper was in Jerusalem, which, of course, was in the area of the tribe of Judah. However, the boundary for the tribe of Benjamin ran very close to Jerusalem, if not actually within the city itself. At any rate, Judah was the main tribe, and more specifically, because the Lord Jesus Christ, the very reason for the existence of Israel, came from that tribe.

KEEP AND SEEK THE COMMANDMENTS OF THE LORD

This was the condition for the blessing of God upon Israel. They were to keep the commandments of the Lord and to seek understanding of these commandments.

These commandments included the entirety of the law of Moses, but more specifically, were centered up in that which we refer to as the Ten Commandments (Ex., Chpt. 20).

To be sure, the law of Moses did not save them, as the law cannot save. In fact, it was what the sacrificial system represented that brought salvation. They were to understand that the sacrificial system pointed to one who was to come, who would pay the full price, and Jesus was that one.

THE LAW

The Ten Commandments part of the law was the standard of the righteousness of God. It was what He demanded of men, and rightly so. As we look at these commandments, they seem simple enough, but the truth is, man in his fallen state has been rendered helpless in the face of obedience. In other words, he simply cannot keep these commandments, no matter how hard he tries. Yet, the Lord placed great stock in the sincere trying. The law covered every aspect of life and living as it regarded the people of Israel. It included everything and excluded nothing. This was the only law on the face of the earth which was given by Jehovah. All other laws and all other nations in the world were man-devised and, therefore, terribly uneven. This put Israel light years, so to speak, ahead of the balance of the nations of the world.

It was when Israel ceased to *keep and seek* that she ultimately lost it all.

THE LAW AND THE MODERN CHRISTIAN

Of course, as is surely known, Jesus fulfilled the law in every capacity when He came. He kept the law perfectly in His life and living, never failing even one time in thought, word, or deed. In fact, He did it all for us, even as our substitutionary man.

He satisfied, as well, every aspect of the broken law by giving Himself as a perfect sacrifice on the Cross in the pouring out of His precious blood, a sacrifice, incidentally, which God readily accepted as payment for all sin, at least for all who will believe (Jn. 3:16).

So, where does that leave the modern Christian and the law? Are the Ten Commandments, the moral law of God, still incumbent upon us as believers?

They certainly are simply because moral law cannot change.

Considering that, does that mean that modern believers should set about to keep the commandments?

To be sure, these commandments must be kept, but not in the way as normally suggested.

WHAT IS THE ANSWER?

The truth is, modern Christians, even Spirit-filled Christians, cannot keep the law of God any better than our Jewish friends of so long ago. We may think we can because we live under the dispensation of grace and because we have the Holy Spirit, but if the truth be known, we are quick to find out that we simply can't do what is demanded of us. As someone has well said, the law is like a mirror, which shows man what he is but gives no power to change what he sees.

So, what is the answer?

The believer is to approach the law in this manner. We are first to understand that Jesus fulfilled the law in every capacity. He is the end of the law! Considering that, we are to place our faith exclusively in Him and what He did for us at the Cross. With that being the case, the Holy Spirit, who works completely within the parameters of the finished work of Christ, will work mightily on our behalf, in effect, keeping the law for us.

In other words, keeping the law should not be a bother for the child of God. It is not the law on which we dwell, but rather faith (Rom. 5:1-2). To be sure, the object of that faith must always be the Cross of Christ because it was there that all victory was won.

THE HOLY SPIRIT

Whatever is done in the heart and life of the believer, it is the Holy Spirit alone who can carry out the task. In other words, the believer—no matter that he is Spirit-filled or not—cannot make himself holy, cannot make himself righteous, and cannot initiate spiritual growth within his heart and life. All of these things must be done by the Holy Spirit.

The key to Him doing all of these things is our faith, but more than all, the correct object of our faith, which must be the Cross.

Regrettably, most modern Christians don't have the faintest idea as to how the Holy Spirit works. Please believe me, without Him, we cannot do anything. Christ through the Holy Spirit lives within our hearts and our lives, and works within our hearts and our lives (Gal. 2:20). However, never forget, the Cross of Christ is the very center of circumference. This is where the victory was won, and this is how the Holy Spirit works.

For the believer to place his faith exclusively in the Cross of Christ and maintain his faith in that finished work, it will garner the action of the Holy Spirit within the believer's life, with the commandments being kept without any thought given as it regards how it is done. Please remember, what is impossible with us *is* possible with the Holy Spirit. He is God!

THE PATTERN

And you, Solomon my son, know you the God of your father, and serve Him with a perfect heart and with a willing mind: for the

LORD *searches all hearts, and understands all the imaginations of the thoughts: if you seek Him, He will be found of you; but if you forsake Him, He will cast you off forever. Take heed now; for the* LORD *has chosen you to build an house for the sanctuary: be strong, and do it. Then David gave to Solomon his son the pattern of the porch, and of the houses thereof, and of the treasuries thereof, and of the upper chambers thereof, and of the inner parlors thereof, and of the place of the mercy seat, And the pattern of all that he had by the Spirit, of the courts of the house of the* LORD, *and of all the chambers round about, of the treasuries of the house of God, and of the treasuries of the dedicated things: Also for the courses of the priests and the Levites, and for all the work of the service of the house of the* LORD, *and for all the vessels of service in the house of the* LORD (I Chron. 28:9-13).

AN OBEDIENT HEART AND A WILLING MIND

Actually, the only thing that one can give to the Lord is an obedient heart with a willing mind. Verse 9 also proclaims the fact that the Lord sees all things and knows all things, past, present, and future. In verse 9 is also one of the greatest promises found in the entirety of the Word of God. Irrespective of the disposition of the individual involved, if the person seeks the Lord with all his heart, the Lord will be found. What a consolation! Conversely, if we turn our backs on the Lord, He will turn His back on us. Consequently, this completely refutes the unscriptural doctrine of unconditional eternal security.

These verses declare that the temple of Solomon was wholly planned by God and an absolutely full pattern of it and its vessels given to David—nothing was left to his or to Solomon's imagination.

THE GREAT PROMISE OF GOD

Beautiful is the promise, if you seek Him, He will be found of you. That is the Word of the Lord, and it is just as true today as it was when it was uttered some 3,000 years ago.

About 400 years later, the great Prophet Jeremiah said something very similar, *"And you shall seek Me, and find Me, when you shall search for Me with all your heart"* (Jer. 29:13).

What a word! This is an unlimited invitation, in effect, saying, "Whosoever will." If anyone wants the Lord and all the things that He alone can do, this passage tells us in no uncertain terms that we can find Him, that is, if we will seek Him.

Why will men lean on the frail arm of other men when they have the Lord to whom they can turn? It is understandable that the world would do such but not at all understandable as it regards the church. Yet, so few earnestly seek the Lord, with almost all seeking that which is constituted by man.

THE PATTERN OF ALL THAT HE HAD BY THE SPIRIT

This was not David's spirit, but rather the Holy Spirit. All of this means that the Holy Spirit guided David in every aspect of the temple, even down to the minutest detail. In other words, none of the pattern was out of David's mind or that of his son Solomon. All of it was of the Lord.

Even the weight of the gold and silver was measured out for the various instruments and sacred vessels.

Everything done on this earth as it pertains to the work of God is done, without exception, through the person, office, and ministry of the Holy Spirit.

Before the Cross, the Holy Spirit was greatly limited as to what He could do. The reason was that the sin debt, which was on the head of every person, could not be removed by the blood of bulls and goats.

Therefore, the Holy Spirit could not come into the hearts and lives of believers during Old Testament times except for short periods of time, and then, only to enable the person to carry out a particular task (Heb. 10:4).

Since the Cross, which atoned for all sin, past, present, and future (at least for all who will believe), the Holy Spirit now comes into the heart and life of the believer at conversion, there to remain forever (Jn. 14:16-17).

Before the Cross, the Holy Spirit dwelt with believers. Now He dwells in believers (Jn. 14:17). This presents a tremendous improvement.

The Holy Spirit would now help David draw the plans for the temple in total detail. Those plans would be given to Solomon for him to construct this edifice. It would be the grandest building ever constructed because it would be the only building in which the Lord would dwell.

THE GOLD

He gave of gold by weight for things of gold, for all instruments of all manner of service; silver also for all instruments of silver by weight, for all instruments of every kind of service: Even the weight for the candlesticks of gold, and for their lamps of gold, by weight for every candlestick, and for the lamps thereof: and for the candlesticks of silver by weight, both for the candlestick, and also for the lamps thereof, according to the use of every candlestick. And by weight he gave gold for the tables of shewbread, for every table; and likewise silver for the tables of silver: Also pure gold for the fleshhooks, and the bowls, and the cups: and for the golden basins he gave gold by weight for every basin; and likewise silver by weight for every basin of silver: And for the altar of incense refined gold by weight; and gold for the pattern of the chariot of the cherubims, that spread out their wings, and covered the ark of the covenant of the LORD. All this, said David, the LORD made me understand in writing by His hand upon me, even all the works of this pattern. And David said to Solomon his son, Be strong and of good courage, and do it: fear not, nor be dismayed: for the LORD God, even my God, will be with you; He will not fail you, nor forsake you, until you have finished all the work for the service of the house of the LORD. And, behold, the courses of the priests and the Levites, even they shall be with you for all the service of the house of God: and there shall be with you for all manner of workmanship every willing skillful man, for any manner of service: also the princes and all the people will be wholly at your commandment (I Chron. 28:14-21).

INSPIRATION

David said that this divine pattern was communicated to him by his being compelled by the hand, or the Spirit, of Jehovah to record it all in writing, which he did! Nothing was left, as stated, to Solomon's or David's genius or taste. All was *"by the Spirit"*; all was divine! David's words to Solomon, as it regarded the charge given to him, were very similar to the charge given to Joshua by none other than the Lord (Josh. 1:9). The closing verses of this chapter are most important because they declare that the temple of Solomon was wholly planned by God, and an absolutely full pattern of it and its vessels was given to David. Nothing was left to his or to Solomon's imagination. As well, these closing verses throw a great light upon the mode of inspiration.

THE DIVINE PATTERN

This appears in verses 12 and 19. Here, David says that this divine pattern was communicated to him by his being compelled by the hand, or the Spirit, of Jehovah to record it all in writing.

These passages, therefore, picture David drawing the pattern of every portion of the temple, great or small, and of every article of its varied ministry, and writing explanatory notes of the drawings. They also picture David dividing the woods and metals to be used and the weight of the several metals. He is seen to do this all when under the inspiration of the Holy Spirit. As well, from this explanation, we are given a view as to how the Bible in its entirety was written.

O the deep, deep love of Jesus,
Vast, unmeasured, boundless, free;
Rolling as a mighty ocean,
In its fullness over me.
Underneath me, all around me,
Is the current of Your love;
Leading onward, leading homeward,
To my glorious rest above.

O the deep, deep love of Jesus,
Spread His praise from shore to shore;
How He loves, ever loves,
Changes never, nevermore,
How He watches o'er His loved ones,
Died to call them all His own;
How for them He intercedes,
Watches o'er them from the throne.

O the deep, deep love of Jesus,
Love of every love the best;
'Tis an ocean vast of blessing,
'Tis a haven sweet of rest,
O the deep, deep love of Jesus,
'Tis a Heaven of Heavens to me;
And it lifts me up to glory,
For it lifts me up to Thee.

THE PALACE IS NOT FOR
MAN, BUT FOR GOD

THE PALACE IS NOT FOR MAN, BUT FOR GOD

"FURTHERMORE DAVID THE KING said unto all the congre-gation, Solomon my son, whom alone God has chosen, is yet young and tender, and the work is great: for the palace is not for man, but for the Lord *God. Now I have prepared with all my might for the house of my God the gold for things to be made of gold, and the silver for things of silver, and the brass for things of brass, the iron for things of iron, and wood for things of wood; onyx stones, and stones to be set, glistering stones, and of divers colors, and all manner of precious stones, and marble stones in abundance. Moreover, because I have set my affection to the house of my God, I have of my own proper good, of gold and silver, which I have given to the house of my God, over and above all that I have prepared for the holy house, Even three thousand talents of gold, of the gold of Ophir, and seven thousand talents of refined silver, to overlay the walls of the houses withal: The gold for things of gold, and the silver for things of silver,*

and for all manner of work to be made by the hands of artificers. And who then is willing to consecrate his service this day unto the LORD? Then the chief of the fathers and princes of the tribes of Israel, and the captains of thousands and of hundreds, with the rulers of the king's work, offered willingly, And gave for the service of the house of God of gold five thousand talents and ten thousand drams, and of silver ten thousand talents, and of brass eighteen thousand talents, and one hundred thousand talents of iron. And they with whom precious stones were found gave them to the treasure of the house of the LORD, by the hand of Jehiel the Gershonite. Then the people rejoiced, for that they offered willingly, because with perfect heart they offered willingly to the LORD: and David the king also rejoiced with great joy" (I Chron. 29:1-9).

IT IS ALL FOR THE LORD

The above verses continue the account of what David said to the whole congregation respecting his son Solomon. David's preparation was never for himself but for God; however, if the Lord is put first, then blessings will come to such an individual (Mat. 6:33).

In today's inflationary dollar, David would have personally given over $40 billion for the construction of the temple (the cost of the temple would be over $1 trillion in today's currency, with much of the cost going to labor).

Our service to God is to always be on a voluntary basis. As well, the Lord accepts the consecration of all, both small and great. As God has freely given to us, will we freely give to Him?

The words *"perfect heart"* specify that the motivation of the people was not one of greed. Proper giving always elicits *"great joy!"*

AFFECTION TO THE HOUSE OF MY GOD

David uttered the words of the heading, and the Holy Spirit sanctioned them. This is David's love, even though the temple was not yet built. He understood that God would dwell in this temple, making it the most unique building on the face of the earth.

Since the Cross, which settled the sin debt, at least for all who will believe, the Holy Spirit now dwells in the hearts and lives of all believers, and does so permanently. What a blessing!

Verse 2 says, *"Now I have prepared with all my might for the house of my God."*

Verse 3 says, *"Moreover, because I have set my affection to the house of my God."*

Verse 3 also says, *"Which I have given to the house of my God."* So, there are three things that David here did. They are:

1. He prepared.

2. He loved.

3. He gave.

If one properly prepares himself toward God, at the same time, he will greatly love the Lord and, as well, will always give to the work of God. Why not, considering what the LORD has given unto us?

WHO IS WILLING TO CONSECRATE?

Verse 5 proclaims David asking this question, *"And who then is willing to consecrate his service this day unto the LORD?"* Several things must be noted about this question.

- Our service to God is always on a voluntary basis.

- God accepts the consecration of all, both small and great.

- This question is a test of faith because God is the one who gave it to us in the first place.

- As God has freely given to us, will we freely give to Him?

OFFERED WILLINGLY

Verse 9 says, *"Then the people rejoiced."*
The tremendous offering given by the people listed in these passages proclaims that which was given by a willing heart to the Lord. Such always elicits tremendous joy. The Holy Spirit says: *"Because with perfect heart they offered willingly to the LORD."*
The words *"perfect heart"* specify that their motivation was not one of greed. Too often the Christian gives in order to receive. This is not really giving. It is more of an investment or

even a gamble. God will have none of it. The Apostle Paul and his tremendous treatment of the grace of giving in II Corinthians, Chapters 7 and 8, extols the abundance of God's blessings that come to the liberal giver; however, He also says that our giving is *"to prove the sincerity of your love"* (II Cor. 8:8). God will accept giving on no other basis.

BLESS THE LORD YOUR GOD

> *Wherefore David blessed the Lord before all the congregation: and David said, Blessed be you, LORD God of Israel our father, forever and ever. Yours, O LORD, is the greatness, and the power, and the glory, and the victory, and the majesty: for all that is in the heaven and in the earth is Yours; Yours is the kingdom, O LORD, and You are exalted as head above all. Both riches and honor come of You, and You reign over all; and in Your hand is power and might; and in Your hand it is to make great, and to give strength unto all. Now therefore, our God, we thank You, and praise Your glorious name. But who am I, and what is my people, that we should be able to offer so willingly after this sort? for all things come of You, and of Your own have we given You. For we are strangers before You, and sojourners, as were all our fathers: our days on the earth are as a shadow, and there is none abiding. O LORD our God, all this store that we have prepared to build You an house for Your holy name comes of Your hand, and is all Your own. I know also, my God, that You try the heart, and have pleasure in uprightness. As for me, in the uprightness of my heart I have willingly offered all*

*these things: and now have I seen with joy Your people, which are present here, to offer willingly unto You. O L*ORD *God of Abraham, Isaac, and of Israel, our fathers, keep this forever in the imagination of the thoughts of the heart of Your people, and prepare their heart unto You: And give unto Solomon my son a perfect heart, to keep Your commandments, Your testimonies, and Your statutes, and to do all these things, and to build the palace, for the which I have made provision. And David said to all the congregation, Now bless the L*ORD *your God. And all the congregation blessed the L*ORD *God of their fathers, and bowed down their heads, and worshipped the L*ORD*, and the king. And they sacrificed sacrifices unto the L*ORD*, and offered burnt offerings unto the L*ORD*, on the morrow after that day, even a thousand bullocks, a thousand rams, and a thousand lambs, with their drink offerings, and sacrifices in abundance for all Israel* (I Chron. 29:10-21).

HUMAN DEPENDENCE ON GOD

The majesty of this prayer includes adoration, acknowledgment of the inherent nature of human dependence, self-humiliation, confession, dedication of all the offerings, and prayer both for the whole people in general and for Solomon in particular. Even though the people gave liberally to the work of God, it was what God had given to them in the first place, as it is with all of us.

It may very well be possible that the stress with which David said, *"I know,"* in verse 17 was because of a special cause. The thought of God as one who *tries the heart* is one often brought out in David's psalms. Most probably, the sacrifices listed in verse 21 were offered on the threshingfloor of Araunah the Jebusite, where the temple would be built. All is ever anchored in Calvary.

All the gold and silver given on this memorable occasion could not purchase redemption of even one soul. This could only be brought about by the precious shed blood of the Lord Jesus Christ. The giving of the people pointed toward Calvary; the temple sight pointed toward Calvary; and the construction of the temple itself would point toward Calvary.

In fact, the entirety of the temple site must have been saturated with blood. To the unspiritual eye, this would have been a gruesome and unacceptable sight. To those who know their Lord and His love for lost mankind, it would speak of redemption so glorious that it would beggar description.

THINE IS THE KINGDOM

This prayer prayed by David even after he had addressed the people was most surely inspired by the Holy Spirit.

He began the prayer by saying, *"Blessed be You,* Lord *God of Israel our father, forever and ever."*

In our petitions to the Lord, we should carefully consider what David did here. He entered into this prayer by blessing the Lord. How ill-mannered it is for believers to begin their petition before the Lord with a shopping list, so to speak, of wants and desires. Such completely ignores the majesty of the Lord and the goodness that He has already given unto us. That's the reason the psalmist said:

"Enter into His gates with thanksgiving, and into His courts with praise: be thankful unto Him, and bless His name" (Ps. 100:4).

Verse 11 is very similar to the prayer prayed by our Lord:

"Our Father who is in heaven, hallowed be Your name. Your kingdom come, Your will be done in earth, as it is in heaven. Give us this day our daily bread. And forgive us our debts, as we forgive our debtors. And lead us not into temptation, but deliver us from evil: for Yours is the kingdom, and the power, and the glory, forever. Amen" (Mat. 6:9-13).

In verse 12, David proclaims the fact that riches and honor come from the Lord and that He reigns over all. He is the One who makes great and gives strength unto all, meaning that everything is in His hands.

WHO AM I?

David now put himself in a place and a position of subservience, which is where he most definitely should have been, and all others as well. Humility is the hallmark of the true child of God. Please allow me to say the following:

It is not possible, I think, for any believer to know and understand humility without first having an understanding of the Cross, both as it refers to salvation and sanctification. While most have an elementary understanding as it refers to salvation, almost all Christians are woefully lacking as it refers to the Cross of Christ and sanctification. Not understanding the Cross as it refers to our everyday life and living before the Lord and the total place and position that it plays in our hearts and lives, a believer is then going to resort to law, whether he or she understands it or not. With that being the case, humility will not be the end result of such action, but rather self-righteousness. The only cure for pride, self-righteousness, etc., is the Cross of Christ. When I say "only," I mean "only." As someone has well said, "The ground is level at the foot of the Cross."

IN THE HAND OF THE LORD

David knew what he was. He knew that everything he had from the Lord was given because of the grace of God. He knew that he merited nothing as far as blessings were concerned and, in fact, merited stern judgment. However, because of the love and grace of God, which were available to David and are available to all others, as well, the sweet singer of Israel had been blessed supremely. So have we!

David plainly said that riches and honor come of the Lord, and He reigns over all. Also, all *"power and might"* are in the hand of the Lord. The Lord, David said, has the power to *"make great"* and *"to give strength unto all."* In that one verse, verse 12, we have the secret of all prosperity, riches, and advancement. It is all in the Lord, even as all things are always all in the Lord.

PROSPERITY

Every believer, at least those who understand the secret of all things, which is Christ and Him crucified, ought to believe

God for prosperity, ought to believe God for blessings, ought to believe God for advancement, and ought to believe God for beautiful, good, and wonderful things to happen to each of us as a child of God. I think we do not expect great things to happen as we should.

Please understand that the economy of the Lord is not tied to Wall Street or the economy of the world in any fashion. God's economy is dependent on nothing!

In view of all of this, the sweet singer of Israel said, *"Now therefore, our God, we thank You, and praise Your glorious name."*

MAKE THE MOST OF THE TIME WE HAVE

The king said, *"For we are strangers before You, and sojourners, as were all our fathers: our days on the earth are as a shadow, and there is none abiding."*

In other words, we don't have long on this earth, and we should make the most of what we have.

Everything should be for the Lord; everything should be from the Lord; and everything should be by the Lord. He should be our life and living 24 hours a day, seven days a week, and that is not only for preachers but, also, for all who speak His name.

THE TRYING OF THE HEART

In the Psalms, a number of times David speaks of the heart being tried by God. The greater the call of God on a heart and life, the greater will be the trial of the heart. It's not that God may know, for He already knows, but that we may know.

Concerning the heart, the great Prophet Jeremiah said:

The heart is deceitful above all things, and desperately wicked: who can know it? (God knows the hopeless corruption of the natural heart, and so He said to Nicodemus that no one, no matter how cultured and moral, can either see or enter into the kingdom of God, unless he is born again). *I the LORD search the heart, I try the reins, even to give every man according to His ways, and according to the fruit of his doings.* (The phrase, 'I the Lord search the heart,' refers to the fact that only God knows the heart. The phrase, 'I try the reins,' refers to the Lord allowing certain particulars to take place, according to the disposition of the individual involved, in order to bring out what is actually there. The Lord, as stated, through omniscience already knows all things, in other words, what is in the heart of man, even before man knows it. However, in order that man not be able to say that he is unjustly judged, the Lord allows events to transpire, uncaused or caused by Him, which always reveal exactly what is in the heart, whether good or bad. This is done in order that the judgment day will be fair and impartial, and that the record of such actions can be shown in black and white to the individual, who, at that time, will be without argument. Therefore, his judgment will be 'according to his ways, and according to the fruit of his doings') (Jer. 17:9-10) (The Expositor's Study Bible).

THE CROSS OF CHRIST

"And they sacrificed sacrifices unto the LORD, and offered burnt offerings unto the LORD, on the morrow after that day, even a thousand bullocks, a thousand rams, and a thousand lambs, with their drink offerings, and sacrifices in abundance for all Israel" (I Chron. 29:21).

These multitudinous sacrifices evidently were offered on the threshingfloor of Araunah the Jebusite, where the temple would be built.

All of this tells us that all is ever anchored in Calvary. All the gold and silver given on this memorable occasion could not purchase the redemption of even one soul. This could only be brought about by the precious shed blood of the Lord Jesus Christ. All of this means that everything done here pointed toward Calvary.

Whenever our worship is anchored in Calvary as verse 22 says, there will always be *"great gladness."*

SOLOMON THE KING

And did eat and drink before the LORD on that day with great gladness. And they made Solomon the son of David king the second time, and anointed him unto the LORD to be the chief governor, and Zadok to be priest. Then Solomon sat on the throne of the LORD as king instead of David his father, and prospered; and all Israel obeyed him. And all the princes, and the mighty men, and all the sons likewise of King David, submitted themselves unto Solomon the king. And the LORD magnified Solomon exceedingly in the sight of all Israel, and bestowed upon him such royal majesty as had not been on any king before him in Israel (I Chron. 29:22-25).

The second anointing has reference to the first anointing, as is outlined in I Kings, Chapter 1. However, this anointing was before the entirety of Israel.

Verse 25 speaks of Solomon, but more particularly, of the greater than Solomon, the Lord Jesus Christ. All of this will come to pass in the coming kingdom age. The Lord magnifies that which He chooses. He does not magnify that which is chosen by man.

THE DOUBLE CONSECRATION

Concerning Solomon on this occasion, Williams says,

This double consecration, Solomon being anointed twice, was necessary because he was divinely assigned to be a type of the greater than Solomon. Two key words unlock the significance of these two crownings.

The key words are *'the altar of burnt offering'* (Chpt. 22:1), and the *'throne of Jehovah'* (Chpt. 29:23).

The first symbolizes grace; the second, glory. The first is connected with Calvary; the second with the millennium. The setting up of the altar of burnt offering on the threshingfloor of Araunah the Jebusite, was followed by the first coronation of Solomon. The completion of the material for the temple occasioned the second crowning. So, with Christ's sacrifice upon Calvary, He is crowned in the heavens; His spiritual temple completed, He will ascend the throne of Jehovah at Jerusalem in the crowning day that will mark the beginning of the kingdom age.

DAVID, THE SON OF JESSE

Thus David the son of Jesse reigned over all Israel. And the time that he reigned over Israel was forty years; seven years reigned he in Hebron, and thirty and three years reigned he in Jerusalem. And he died in a good old age, full of days, riches, and honor: and Solomon his son reigned in his stead. Now the acts of David the king, first and last, behold, they are written in the book of Samuel the seer, and in the book of Nathan the prophet, and in the book of Gad the seer, With all his reign and his might, and the times that went over him, and over Israel, and over all the kingdoms of the countries (I Chron. 29:26-30).

So concluded the life of one of the greatest men of God who ever lived.

David wrote more than half of the psalms, and he was given the plans for the temple, which would be the grandest building ever constructed by the hand of man. Above all, he would be the ancestor of the incarnation, of Whom the Son of David would be named. His name is the first human name in the

New Testament (Mat. 1:1). It is, as well, the last human name in the New Testament (Rev. 22:16).

And yet, David's greatest time is yet to come. I speak of the coming kingdom age when he will rule and reign over all of Israel, directly under the Lord Jesus Christ (Ezek. 37:24-25).

And can it be that I should gain an interest
In the Saviour's blood?
Died He for me, who caused His pain?
For me who Him to death pursued?

Amazing love! How can it be
That Thou, my God, should die for me?
Amazing love! How can it be
That Thou, my God, should die for me?

Tis mystery all! Th' Immortal dies:
Who can explore His strange design?
In vain the firstborn seraph tries
To sound the depths of love divine.
Tis mercy all! Let earth adore,
Let angel minds inquire no more.
Tis mercy all! Let earth adore,
Let angel minds inquire no more.

He left His Father's throne above,
So free, so infinite His grace.
Emptied Himself of all but love,
And bled for Adam's helpless race.
Tis mercy all, immense and free;
For O my God, it found out me!
Tis mercy all, immense and free;
For O my God, it found out me!

Long my imprisoned spirit lay,
Fast bound in sin and nature's night;
Thine eye diffused a quickening ray,
I woke, the dungeon flamed with light;
My chains fell off, my heart was free,
I rose, went forth, and followed Thee.
My chains fell off, my heart was free,
I rose, went forth, and followed Thee.

No condemnation now I dread;
Jesus and all in Him is mine!
Alive in Him, my living head,
And clothed in righteousness divine,
Bold I approach the eternal throne,
And claim the crown, through Christ my own.
Bold I approach the eternal throne,
And claim the crown, through Christ my own.

BUILD THE HOUSE

BUILD THE HOUSE

"AND SOLOMON DETERMINED TO build an house for the name of the Lord, *and an house for his kingdom. And Solomon told out threescore and ten thousand men to bear burdens, and fourscore thousand to hew in the mountain, and three thousand and six hundred to oversee them. And Solomon sent to Huram the king of Tyre, saying, As you did deal with David my father, and did send him cedars to build him an house to dwell therein, even so deal with me. Behold, I build an house to the name of the* Lord *my God, to dedicate it to Him, and to burn before Him sweet incense, and for the continual shewbread, and for the burnt offerings morning and evening, on the Sabbaths, and on the new moons, and on the solemn feasts of the* Lord *our God. This is an ordinance forever to Israel. And the house which I build is great: for great is our God above all gods. But who is able to build Him an house, seeing the heaven and heaven of heavens cannot contain Him? who am I then, that I should build Him an house, save only to burn sacrifice before Him? Send me now therefore a man cunning to work in gold, and in silver, and in brass, and in iron, and in purple, and crimson, and blue, and who can skill to grave with the cunning men who are with*

me in Judah and in Jerusalem, whom David my father did provide. Send me also cedar trees, fir trees, and algum trees, out of Lebanon: for I know that your servants can skill to cut timber in Lebanon; and, behold, my servants shall be with your servants, Even to prepare me timber in abundance: for the house which I am about to build shall be wonderful great. And, behold, I will give to your servants, the hewers who cut timber, twenty thousand measures of beaten wheat, and twenty thousand measures of barley, and twenty thousand baths of wine, and twenty thousand baths of oil" (II Chron. 2:1-10).

TWO STRUCTURES

In essence, Solomon wanted to build two structures, the temple and a royal residence for himself.

The wording of verse 1 proclaims to us that Solomon's determination was even more than the prompting to do so by his father David. The Holy Spirit was, in fact, now helping him. A total of 153,600 men were pressed into service for the construction of the temple. These were all foreigners, Gentiles, and actually prisoners of war, justly condemned to hard labor for life. David could easily have put these men to death as he might justly have done, for when they were captured, they had been attempting to kill David and destroy Israel and the God of Israel. So, David allowing these people to remain alive was an act of mercy on his part. As well, any one of these individuals could have subscribed to the God of Abraham, Isaac, and Jacob by submitting to the law of Moses and to circumcision. They would have then become free men. Possibly, some of them did this.

The Hiram of verse 3 was not the same Hiram of David's day, but the son of the Hiram of II Samuel 5:11.

The mention of these three particulars portrays Christ. The *"sweet incense"* speaks of His glorious presence. The *"continual shewbread"* speaks of His continual life, for Jesus is the Bread of Life. The *"burnt offerings"* speak of His glorious sacrifice at Calvary that would forever atone for the sins of man in their redemption.

THE GREATNESS OF GOD

The testimony of Solomon as to the greatness of God above the heathen entities of surrounding nations is a witness to his boldness of testimony. He did not flinch from proclaiming the greatness of God over the insignificance of the god of Tyre, which was the capital of Lebanon, the realm over which King Hiram reigned. Solomon's statement of verse 6 actually refers back to the time that David desired to build a house for the Lord (I Chron., Chpt. 17), and the Lord, in effect, told David, "I do not want or need your house, and furthermore, I will build you a house" (I Chron. 17:10). The major problem of the church is that it tries to build the Lord a house. We are the ones who need the house, and that house is Jesus.

It is remarkable that in Solomon's letter nearly two-thirds of it extol the God of glory, with only about one-third itemizing his request. This house would be *"wonderful great"* only because the Lord would occupy the structure; otherwise, it would be just another house.

As stated in II Chronicles 2, a *"measure"* equals about three gallons, while a *"bath"* equals about six gallons.

BUILDING THE HOUSE

Previously stated in the commentary of I Chronicles, the Lord gave the plans in toto to David as it regarded what the temple would be. Nothing was left to chance or guess, with every single part of the structure designed by the Holy Spirit and then given to David, who was to give it to Solomon for the temple to be built. David was instructed that he could not build the temple for a variety of reasons. His son Solomon would put up this structure.

It would be the only building in the world where God would dwell, in fact, in the Holy of Holies, between the mercy seat and the cherubim. To be sure, the building within itself was not large, but considering the way that it was to be constructed, even as we shall see, the cost would probably be in the neighborhood of a trillion dollars if tabulated according to today's currency.

HOLY

Considering that not even the sound of a hammer was to be heard on a temple site while construction was taking place, several things were demanded (I Ki. 6:7).

Every single part of the temple, whatever it was, whether hewed stones or whether things much smaller, all and without exception had to be prepared off the temple site. This catapulted the cost to an astronomical level, as would be obvious. There were 153,600 men employed for seven and a half years (II Chron. 2:17-18).

The manner of construction was because of the Holy Spirit. This would be where God would dwell and, in fact, it would be occupied by the third person of the Trinity, the Holy Spirit. Even presently, when the Spirit of God moves in certain ways, one does not want to make a sound for fear of offending the Lord. Of course, the Holy Spirit moves in many and varied ways, but at least one of those ways pertains to all human activities stopping, especially if it generates noise of any kind.

A PERSONAL EXPERIENCE

In our Thanksgiving Campmeeting conducted at Family Worship Center in Baton Rouge, Louisiana, a most thrilling thing took place on the Saturday night of that meeting. It was in November 2007.

The service concluded, and we had experienced a mighty moving of the Holy Spirit in various ways. I stepped up to the pulpit and dismissed the people, but strangely enough, no one left. Then it was like a holy hush settled down over the sanctuary.

I sat down in a chair on the platform and began to lead the people in worship choruses.

For over an hour, no one moved, with the exception of getting out of their seats and going to the altar. The Holy Spirit was present in such a way that no one wanted to make a sound for fear of offending Him. Some few of you know what I mean. In a sense, this is what was happening at the temple site where the building would ultimately come under construction. It was to be a house in which the Holy Spirit would dwell. Due to the Cross, He now dwells within our hearts and lives and does so permanently. That includes every believer (I Cor. 3:16).

THE THREE PARTICULARS OF THE TEMPLE

Those three are:

1. Sweet incense
2. Shewbread
3. Burnt offerings

The incense had to do with the golden altar, which sat immediately in front of the veil, which led into the Holy of Holies. Other than the side rooms of the temple, the main temple itself had only two rooms—the Holy of Holies, and the Holy Place where the tables of shewbread were placed, five to each side, and the lampstands, five to each side. There was only one golden altar, or as it was sometimes referred, the altar of incense.

Twice a day, the priests would come into the Holy Place, bringing coals of fire from the brazen altar, with these coals deposited on the golden altar. Over those coals was poured the incense, which filled the Holy Place with a cloud. This was a type of the intercession of Christ that is carried on presently in heaven on behalf of every saint, and has been carried on since the time of the ascension of Christ. The intercession of Christ needed by every believer, and carried on for every believer, makes possible our prayers and our petitions.

THE SHEWBREAD

As it regards the shewbread, there were 10 tables in the Holy Place, five to one side and five to the other, each carrying 12 loaves, which were consumed by the priests every Sabbath, with fresh loaves taking their place. This was a type of Christ as the Bread of Life.

The golden lampstands were a type of Christ as the light of the world. As stated, there were 10 of these lampstands, five to each side.

Every morning at 9 a.m., the priests would come in and trim the wicks of the lamps and replenish the oil. They would do the same thing at 3 p.m. These were the times, as well, that coals of fire were brought from the brazen altar and placed on the golden altar of incense.

Incidentally, no sacrifices were to be offered on this golden altar, only the incense. To have done so would have repudiated what the brazen altar represented, which was the Cross of Christ.

THE BURNT OFFERINGS

As should be obvious, as with the tabernacle that preceded the temple, every ceremony and every ritual, as it regarded the temple, represented Christ in His atoning work, His mediatorial work, or His intercessory work. When Christ came, neither the temple nor its appointments was needed anymore.

The burnt offerings were actually the core of all that the temple represented. Most of the time, when burnt offerings were offered, they were preceded by a sin offering.

As previously stated, the sin offering portrayed Christ taking all the sins of the sinner, while the whole burnt offering portrayed Christ giving His perfection to the sinner.

The burnt offerings were a type of Christ and what He would do in the giving of Himself on the Cross of Calvary. This was the heartbeat of the temple, the very reason for its existence.

THE CROSS

While, of course, the Holy of Holies, one might say, was the most important part of the temple because it was where God dwelt, still, the Holy of Holies could not be reached except by sacrifice, with the blood applied to the mercy seat. Likewise, presently, the Lord cannot be reached in any capacity unless it is by and through Jesus Christ and what He did at the Cross. The temple is a perfect example of that (Jn. 16:23-24).

Once a year, which was the Great Day of Atonement, the high priest went into the Holy of Holies. He had to go in alone. He would take the blood of the sacrifice and apply it to the mercy seat, actually doing such twice, once for himself and then the second time for Israel.

This portrays in perfect type that the throne of God, of which the Holy of Holies was a type, could not be reached and, in fact, cannot be reached, except by the means of the Cross. That's the reason we constantly state that Christ is the source of all things that we receive from God, while the Cross is the means by which these things are done, all superintended by the Holy Spirit (Eph. 2:13-18).

THE WORK

Then Huram the king of Tyre answered in writing, which he sent to Solomon, Because the LORD has loved His people, He has made you king over them. Huram said moreover, Blessed be the LORD God of Israel, who made heaven and earth, who has given to David the king a wise son, endued with prudence and understanding, who might build an house for the LORD, and an house for His kingdom. And now I have sent a cunning man, endued with understanding, of Huram my father's, The son of a woman of the daughters of Dan, and his father was a man of Tyre, skillful to work in gold, and in silver, in brass, in iron, in stone, and in timber, in purple, in blue, and in fine linen, and in crimson; also to grave any manner of graving, and to find out every device which shall be put to him, with your cunning men, and with the cunning men of my lord David your father. Now therefore the wheat, and the barley, the oil, and the wine, which my lord has spoken of, let him send unto his servants: And we will cut wood out of Lebanon, as much as you shall need: and we will bring it to you in floats by sea to Joppa; and you shall carry it up to Jerusalem. And Solomon numbered all the strangers who were in the land of Israel, after the numbering wherewith David his father had numbered them; and they were found an hundred and fifty thousand and three thousand and six hundred. And he set threescore and ten thousand of them to be bearers of burdens, and fourscore thousand to be hewers in the mountain, and three thousand and six hundred overseers to set the people a work (II Chron. 2:11-18).

THE ONE TRUE GOD

Verse 11 presents a testimony to the indirect influences on surrounding nations of the knowledge of the one true Creator – God i.e., ruler-God, who was domiciled by special revelation and oracle with Israel (Rom. 3:2). Even when nations near were bitter foes, they often feared Israel's God.

Two buildings were to be constructed, a palace for Solomon, which, in essence, would be the center of government, and the temple. There is no doubt that the Lord greatly blessed Hiram and the kingdom of Tyre for their willingness to help as it regarded this work for the Lord.

As it regards verse 16, the distance from Joppa to Jerusalem was about 34 miles.

HIRAM, THE KING OF TYRE

It is spelled *"Hiram"* in II Samuel, Chapter 5, and in I Kings, and is probably the better spelling. As we have seen in the first part of this chapter, Solomon had written Hiram a beautiful letter portraying the glory of Christ. Hiram now answered him.

It should be understood that this was not the Hiram of David's day, but rather his son.

Verse 12 has this heathen king proclaiming the greatness of the Lord by saying, *"Blessed be the LORD God of Israel, who made heaven and earth."* This heathen had more spiritual sense than the majority of so-called christianized America and Canada, who claim evolution as the maker of such. In effect, Hiram stated that he was honored to have a part in this house of God that was to be built. Hiram and the kingdom of Tyre would, no doubt, be greatly blessed because of their participation in this great work of God.

BLESSING

Anything that is truly of the Lord carries with it great blessing. If this heathen prince had enough sense to understand the blessing of such participation, surely modern Christians can understand the same. The truth is, and sadly so, the majority of modern Christendom supports that which is really not of God, which means that no blessing accompanies such efforts.

In all of the earth of that day, what Solomon was doing was of God; consequently, any participation in that work brought blessing.

For instance, when Solomon allowed the Gentiles who were prisoners of war to help in the building of the temple, in essence, he made them fellow workers with himself in the building of this great structure. This forms a picture of Christ, who saves men and makes them captives, allowing us to be fellow laborers in the building of His great spiritual temple. What an honor to be able to work for the Lord in any capacity in the construction of this holy edifice.

WHAT IS THE TRUE WORK OF GOD PRESENTLY?

Pure and simple, it is the Message of the Cross. This is what the Holy Spirit is presently saying, I believe, to the churches. In effect, that has always been the true work of God and, in fact, there has never been any other as there cannot be any other. So, the question presently poses itself:

How many modern preachers are preaching the Cross? Paul said,

For after that in the wisdom of God the world by wisdom knew not God (man's puny wisdom, even the best he has to offer, cannot come to know God in any manner), *it pleased God by the foolishness of preaching* (preaching the Cross) *to save them who believe.* (Paul is not dealing with the art of preaching here, but with what is preached.) *For the Jews require a sign* (the sign of the Messiah taking the throne and making Israel a great nation once again), *and the Greeks seek after wisdom* (they thought that such solved the human problem; however, if it did, why were they ever seeking after more wisdom?): *But we preach Christ crucified* (this is the foundation of the Word of God and, thereby, of salvation), *unto the Jews a stumblingblock* (the Cross was the stumblingblock), *and unto the Greeks foolishness* (both found it difficult to accept as God a dead man hanging on a Cross, for such Christ was to them);

CHRIST, THE POWER OF GOD

But unto them who are called (refers to those who accept the call, for the entirety of mankind is invited [Jn. 3:16; Rev. 22:17]), *both Jews and Greeks* (actually stands for both 'Jews and Gentiles'), *Christ the Power of God* (what He did at the Cross atoned for all sin, thereby, making it possible for the Holy Spirit to exhibit His power within our lives), *and the wisdom of God.* (This wisdom devised a plan of salvation that pardoned guilty men and at the same time vindicated and glorified the justice of God, which stands out as the wisest and most remarkable plan of all time) (I Cor. 1:21-24) (The Expositor's Study Bible).

Paul admits that the preaching of the Cross is foolishness to the world; nevertheless, the Cross must be preached because this is the only manner in which men can be saved. In other words, as we have repeatedly stated, Christ is the source of all things that come from God, and the Cross is the means by which these things are given to us, all superintended by the Holy Spirit (Rom. 8:2; I Cor. 1:17-18; Gal. 6:14).

The sad truth is, at this present time, not many preachers are preaching the Cross. There are a few who preach the Cross as it regards salvation, and thank God for that; however, there are almost none who are preaching the Cross as it regards sanctification, in other words, how we live for God.

Why?

THE PREACHING OF THE CROSS AS IT REGARDS OUR LIFE AND LIVING

The modern church, and I speak of those who claim to truly believe the Bible, knows next to nothing about the Cross of Christ as it regards our daily living for God. In the thinking of most preachers, after salvation, the Cross is forgotten. As a result, the church stumbles from one scheme to the other, trying to find victory. As there is no salvation outside of the Cross, likewise, there is no victory outside of the Cross. Regrettably, as the world tries to save itself outside of the Cross of Christ, the church tries to sanctify itself outside of the Cross of Christ. Neither is successful, as neither can be successful.

What does it mean to preach the Cross as it regards sanctification?

Paul said, *"Christ sent me not to baptize, but to preach the Gospel: not with wisdom of words, lest the Cross of Christ should be made of none effect"* (I Cor. 1:17).

As we've already stated in previous study, in this one verse, the apostle tells us what the Gospel actually is. Please understand that the great apostle was not addressing salvation in this statement, but rather sanctification. To preach the Cross as it regards sanctification simply means that the preacher of the gospel is to proclaim the fact that the Cross of Christ must ever be the object of our faith. This means that the Cross alone is the means by which we receive all things from the Lord. It is the Holy Spirit who gives us all of these things, but He does everything by the means of the Cross. In other words, it is the Cross of Christ that makes it legally possible to do all the things for us that He does. Sadly, however, there is an argument regarding that.

IS IT WHO JESUS WAS OR WHAT JESUS DID?

Generally, those who ask this question are denigrating the Cross. In other words, they do not want to make the Cross the sole object of their faith or play any part at all in their sanctification. So, they try to divide Christ from the Cross, claiming that the Cross is of little consequence and that the emphasis must be placed on who Christ was and is, namely the Son of God.

The answer to that is simple! It is both who He is and what He did. No one else but Jesus Christ, the Son of God, could have carried out this great work of redemption. No angel could have done so, and no human being could have done so, only Christ.

John addressed this by saying:

"In the beginning was the Word, and the Word was with God, and the Word was God" (Jn. 1:1).

This plainly tells us that Jesus Christ was and is God from eternity past to eternity future.

The great apostle then said, *"And the Word was made flesh, and dwelt among us, (and we beheld His glory, the glory as of the only begotten of the Father,) full of grace and truth"* (Jn. 1:14).

Why was the Word made flesh, which speaks of the incarnation of Christ, God becoming man?

THE CROSS

We are given that answer when John the Baptist introduced Christ. He said:

"Behold the Lamb of God, who takes away the sin of the world" (Jn. 1:29).

This tells us that God became man and did so for the purpose of going to the Cross, hence, John addressing Jesus as *"the Lamb of God."*

The short phrase, *"Lamb of God,"* had reference to the untold millions of lambs that had been offered up in sacrifice even from the first page of human history, all symbolic of Christ and what He would do for us at the Cross. Hence, the Holy Spirit, through John the Baptist, referred to Christ as the Lamb of God.

In other words, God became man for the express purpose of going to the Cross and, thereby, redeeming mankind from the terrible bondage of sin. He would give Himself as a perfect sacrifice, which God the Father would accept, thereby, atoning for all sin, past, present, and future, at least for those who will believe (Jn. 3:16).

THE SACRIFICE

Jesus Christ has always been God. He did not suddenly become God in the incarnation. As John 1:1 states, He was God from eternity past and will be God to eternity future. However, the answer to the great question is this:

The mere fact of Him being God, in other words, who He was, did not save anyone. While it was absolutely necessary that He be God, which He was, in order for men to be redeemed, still, that mere fact alone was insufficient for salvation. For salvation to be carried out, which includes sanctification, in other words, all that we receive from the Lord and all that we are in the Lord, it was absolutely necessary that God would become man for the sole purpose of going to the Cross. That was why He came. So, it was not only who He was but, as well, what He did, which refers to the Cross, which alone gives salvation upon faith.

It is absolutely impossible, at least with any degree of honesty, to read the Bible and not see that the central core of the Word of God is Jesus Christ and Him crucified.

In fact, in Old Testament times, every lamb that was offered up, and millions were, all typified Christ and what He would do for us at the Cross. Therefore, to denigrate the Cross in any capacity is to misunderstand the entire scope of the Word of God and the plan of redemption. When the Cross is taken out of Christianity, there is nothing left but a vapid philosophy. Regrettably, that is exactly what is presently being done. Christianity is being degenerated to the mere whims of man.

Oh Jesus, King most wonderful,
Thou conqueror renowned;
Thou sweetness most ineffable,
In whom all joys are found;

When once You visit the heart,
Then truth begins to shine;
Then earthly vanities depart,
Then kindles love divine.

Jesus! Your mercies are untold,
Through each returning day;
Your love exceeds a thousand fold
Whatever we can say.

May every heart confess Your name,
And ever You adore;
And seeking You itself in flame
And seek You more and more.

You may our tongues forever bless;
You may we love alone:
And ever in our lives express
The image of Your own.

CHAPTER 8

THE BEGINNING OF
CONSTRUCTION

THE BEGINNING OF CONSTRUCTION

"THEN SOLOMON BEGAN TO build the house of the Lord at Jerusalem in Mount Moriah, where the LORD appeared unto David his father, in the place that David had prepared in the threshingfloor of Ornan the Jebusite. And he began to build in the second day of the second month, in the fourth year of his reign" (II Chron. 3:1-2).

THE THRESHINGFLOOR

This is the first mention of Mount Moriah since Genesis 22:2. It is never mentioned after this. It is believed that this is where Abraham was to offer up Isaac.

"The threshingfloor of Ornan the Jebusite" presented a place of judgment, which spoke of the destroying angel (II Sam. 24:16). It was now turned into a place of blessing, all by the grace of God.

It is believed that Solomon was 20 years old when he began to reign and 24 years of age when he began construction on the temple. He reigned for 40 years, dying at 60 years of age. No doubt, the Lord would have allowed him to live much longer but for his wrong direction in his last years.

THE BEGINNING OF CONSTRUCTION

I Kings 6:1 states that the beginning of the construction of the temple was some 480 years from the time of the exodus.

Some say this is a corrupted text, with some of the older manuscripts omitting the time frame. In fact, it has never been settled as to exactly how long the period of the judges actually was; however, it is my opinion that the number given in I Kings 6:1 (480 years) is correct.

Their beginning to build constituted the greatest building project in the history of man. In this building, God would dwell, and yet, even as Solomon has said, *"The heaven and heaven of heavens cannot contain You"* (I Ki. 8:27), much less this building.

Nevertheless, this building was designed by the Lord, with its design, down to the minutest detail, being given to David. David then gave the design to his son Solomon, and now the structure was beginning to be built.

Israel was the only nation at this time on the face of the earth who knew Jehovah. This means they were monotheistic, the worshippers of one God, namely Jehovah. All the other nations of the world were polytheistic, meaning they worshipped many gods, in reality, demon spirits. In view of the fact that God was with Israel, this means that they were light years ahead of every other nation on the earth. It was sin that brought them down, and it is sin that will bring anyone down if the sin remains unconfessed and, thereby, unforgiven and forsaken.

THE DESIGN

> *Now these are the things wherein Solomon was instructed for the*
> *building of the house of God. The length by cubits after the first*
> *measure was threescore cubits, and the breadth twenty cubits.*
> *And the porch that was in the front of the house, the length*
> *of it was according to the breadth of the house, twenty cubits,*
> *and the height was an hundred and twenty: and he overlaid it*
> *within with pure gold. And the greater house he cieled with fir*
> *tree, which he overlaid with fine gold, and set thereon palm trees*
> *and chains. And he garnished the house with precious stones*
> *for beauty: and the gold was gold of Parvaim. He overlaid also*
> *the house, the beams, the posts, and the walls thereof, and the*
> *doors thereof, with gold; and graved cherubims on the walls*
> (II Chron. 3:3-7).

THE MEASUREMENTS

The length and width of the house here given pertained to the Holy Place and the Holy of Holies. The entire length was 90 feet, and the width was 30 feet; however, this pertained only to the temple proper. Many rooms were also built on each side.

The height is definitely a copyist error in one of the old manuscripts. This would make the temple 180 feet high – twice as high as it was long. In I Kings 6:2, it states that the height was 30 cubits, or 45 feet, counting 18 inches to the cubit. This would be normal for the highest part of the temple and for the three stories of chambers (I Ki. 6:8).

The *"gold"* signified the deity of Christ, with every part of the temple, in fact, portraying Christ in His atoning, mediatorial, or intercessory work.

Everything about the house was designed by the Holy Spirit, even down to the minutest detail. It had to be adhered to strictly.

The *"cherubims"* spoke of God's holiness.

The *"palm trees"* of verse 5 spoke of the perfect rest found only in Christ, with the *"chains"* of that verse speaking of the never-ceasing link of the child of God with the Lord Jesus Christ.

THE DIMENSIONS OF THE HOUSE

As stated, the structure was 90 feet long. The first room, the Holy Place, was 60 feet long, while the smaller room, which was the Holy of Holies where the ark of the covenant was kept and where God dwelt, was 30 feet long and 30 feet wide.

It should be observed that the great brazen altar, which was a type of Christ and what He would do at the Cross, was, as well, 30 feet wide and 30 feet long. This means that the grace of God through the sacrifice was just as great as the power of God as it pertained to the Holy of Holies.

PURE GOLD

As is here obvious, there was gold in abundance in Solomon's temple. Oddly enough, in the millennial temple described in Ezekiel, Chapters 40 through 48, there is no record that there is any gold whatsoever in that temple. Why the difference?

Gold in the Old Testament, at least as it regarded the tabernacle and the temple, referred to deity. In the coming kingdom age, Christ will be present personally, so there will be no need for gold in the millennial temple. As someone has well said, "What would be the use? Jesus will outshine them all."

The temple of Solomon was a forepicture of the millennial glory of Christ as Melchizedek, but only a forepicture. The tabernacle in the wilderness set out our Lord's grace as Saviour.

Nothing was left to the imagination of Moses in the building of the tabernacle or of Solomon in the building of the temple. Grace was expressed by the tabernacle; glory by the temple. As silver is representative of grace, therefore, it was prominent in the tabernacle. Gold, as stated, spoke of deity and glory, hence, it was prominent in the temple. The tabernacle spoke of access to God; the temple of fellowship with God.

The first building (the tabernacle, in actuality, a tent) pictured Christ in His first advent; the latter building (the temple) pictured Christ in His second advent. The first structure had sand for a floor; the second, gold. The first was a tent; the second, a temple. However, whether a tent or a temple, the materials, the vessels, and all the gathered wealth of each were precious and uttered His praise.

THE GLORY OF GOD

Both the tabernacle and the temple spoke of fellowship with God, which can only come through the atonement of Christ. In other words, it's the Cross that makes it all possible.

Both Solomon and the temple pictured Christ's glorious kingdom over the earth.

Solomon in his glory, riches, and wisdom set out the person of Christ.

The temple symbolized the nature of Christ—with gold prefiguring His deity and cedar His humanity—but all had grace and atonement as its foundation, for this building of glory was built upon the threshingfloor of Araunah the Jebusite.

PRECIOUS STONES

Verse 6 says, *"And he garnished the house with precious stones for beauty."*

This explains what was done with the many precious stones and gems of various colors that David had gathered to beautify the temple (I Chron. 29:2).

This must have been a beautiful sight to behold. The *"precious stones"* spoke of the redeemed. *"And they shall be Mine, says the Lord of Hosts, in that day when I make up My jewels"* (Mal. 3:17).

Verse 7 says, *"And graved cherubims on the walls."* The *"cherubims"* spoke of God's holiness. The *"palm trees"* spoke of rest, which we can only have in Christ. The *"chains"* spoke of the never-ceasing link of the child of God to the Lord Jesus Christ.

God is a thrice-holy God; consequently, the cherubims are living creatures that stand continually before the throne of God in heaven and cry unceasingly, *"Holy, Holy, Holy, Lord God Almighty, which was, and is, and is to come"* (Rev. 4:8).

THE CHERUBIMS

And he made the most holy house, the length whereof was according to the breadth of the house, twenty cubits, and the breadth thereof twenty cubits: and he overlaid it with fine gold, amounting to six hundred talents (one and a half billion dollars in today's currency). *And the weight of the nails was fifty shekels of gold. And he overlaid the upper chambers with gold. And in the most holy house he made two cherubims of image work, and overlaid them with gold. And the wings of the cherubims were twenty cubits long: one wing of the one cherub was five cubits, reaching to the wall of the house: and the other wing was likewise five cubits, reaching to the wing of the other cherub. And one wing of the other cherub was five cubits, reaching to the wall of the house: and the other wing was five cubits also, joining to the wing of the other cherub. The wings of these cherubims spread themselves forth twenty cubits* (30 feet): *and they stood on their feet, and their faces were inward. And he made the veil of blue, and purple, and crimson, and fine linen, and wrought cherubims thereon* (II Chron. 3:8-14).

RIGHTEOUSNESS

"The most holy house" was actually the Holy of Holies, which contained the ark of the covenant. It seems that even the nails were made of pure gold. As it regards the word *"inward"* used in verse 13, there is some indication in the Hebrew that, as used here, it meant "toward the house," in other words, "outward."

In Moses' tabernacle, the cherubim looked down upon the blood-sprinkled mercy seat, for with them being under the reign of sin and death, only there could their eyes rest with satisfaction all around. However, here, the new cherubim looked *outward* upon a kingdom governed in righteousness by the King of righteousness.

The *"veil of blue"* signified that Christ came from heaven.

The *"purple"* signified that Christ is the king.

The *"crimson"* signified His shed blood on the Cross of Calvary, which was necessary in order that man be redeemed.

The *"fine linen"* signified the perfect righteousness of Christ.

CHERUBIMS

The cherubims, as stated, signified the holiness of our Lord. The veil of the temple is described here as being like that in the tabernacle of Moses. It is not mentioned in I Kings at all. In I Kings 6:31, the Holy Spirit records the fact that there were doors made of olivewood between the most Holy Place and the Holy Place. It does not mention the veil. In this passage, it mentions the veil but does not mention the doors. Quite possibly, the veil hung immediately behind the doors; therefore, when the doors were opened, the veil could remain and continue to hide the Holy of Holies from inquisitive stares.

THE HOLY OF HOLIES

"The most holy house" referred, as stated, to the Holy of Holies where the ark of the covenant was kept. It was the smaller of the

two rooms of the main part of the temple. It was 30 feet square and was overlaid with pure gold (I Ki. 6:20). The Scripture says the amount of gold was *"six hundred talents."* As it regards the price of gold today, there would have been nearly a billion dollars worth of gold in this one room.

The flooring, the ceiling, the walls, the ornamentation, the costly stones, the precious wood, the gold, the brass, the carved cherubim, the veils, the two pillars, and all the vessels of the house, together with its golden doors and the dedicated treasures, all pictured the glories, the perfections, the graces, the ministries, the activities, and the offices of Christ in His second advent and millennial reign.

THE NAILS

Verse 9 says, *"And the weight of the nails was fifty shekels of gold."*

This means that the total cost of all the nails was roughly $500,000 in today's currency. How many nails there were, we aren't told.

It is so beautiful how the grace of the Holy Spirit drew attention to the nails used in the construction of this great temple. He does not overlook such small and simple things when detailing all these dazzling splendors. He alone saw them, for they were hidden, but they held everything together and are remembered and named by God.

Were a golden lampstand to speak slightingly of the little golden nail (as some great preachers attempt to treat a junior

Sunday school teacher), the nail could reply that it was also formed of pure gold and had an indispensible office in the structure of this great house of God.

THE CHERUBIM

The Scripture says, *"And in the most holy house, he made two cherubims of image work, and overlaid them with gold."*

These two cherubim were very large, with their wings reaching across the width of the most Holy Place—30 feet. Each wing was five cubits or seven and one-half feet long. The outer ones touched the wall of the house, while the inner ones touched each other. Thus, the two cherubim with their four wings outstretched took the whole width of the room. They were completely covered with gold, and they stood on their feet, which were like those of a calf (Ezek. 1:7).

The latter portion of verse 13 says, *"And their faces were inward."*

The word *inward,* as it is here used, in the Hebrew means, "toward the house," in other words, "outward," and should have been translated accordingly.

AN AWESOME SIGHT

There is no way that the mind of man can grasp how the Holy of Holies must have looked, with these huge cherubim with their outstretched wings covering the entirety of the room and all being overlaid with gold. Even though this was only symbolic of the reality, which was in heaven, still, it must have been an awesome sight.

How wonderful will it be when at long last we stand before the throne of God and hear the cherubim and the seraphim (Isa. 6:1-8) cry, *"Holy, Holy, Holy, Lord God Almighty, which was, and is, and is to come"* (Rev. 4:8).

The cherubim in Moses' tabernacle looked down on the mercy seat and the shed blood because the work was not yet finished. Now, and we speak of Solomon's temple, the cherubim looked outward upon a finished work of the grace and glory of God.

THE PILLARS

Also he made before the house two pillars of thirty and five cubits high, and the chapiter that was on the top of each of them was five cubits. And he made chains, as in the oracle, and put them on the heads of the pillars; and made an hundred pomegranates, and put them on the chains. And he reared up the pillars before the temple, one on the right hand, and the other on the left; and called the name of that on the right hand Jachin, and the name of that on the left Boaz (II Chron. 3:15-17).

Counting the chapiters, the pillars were 60 feet tall. The *"chains"* typified our union with Christ. The *"pomegranates"* typified the fruit of the Spirit. Actually, the two pillars did not hold up anything. They were strictly for ornamentation and signified believers (Rev. 3:12).

The name Jachin means "he shall establish." The name Boaz means "in it is strength." The actual meaning is "believers shall be established in the strength of the Lord."

THE OVERCOMER

As it regards His message to the church at Philadelphia, Jesus said, *"Him who overcomes will I make a pillar in the temple of my God* (the 'overcomer' is the one who trusts explicitly in Christ and what He did for us at the Cross), *and he shall go no more out* (refers to a constant position in the presence of God): *and I will write upon him the name of My God, and the name of the city of My God, which is New Jerusalem, which comes down out of heaven from My God: and I will write upon him My new name.* (At the Cross, Christ identified with our sin by suffering its penalty. Now He identifies with our most excellent blessing, as He is the source of all.) *He who has an ear, let him hear what the Spirit says unto the churches* (Rev. 3:12-13) (The Expositor's Study Bible).

The Holy Spirit is saying that we must preach and teach, and we must believe with all of our hearts the message of Jesus Christ and Him crucified.

As we've already stated, the pillars sat right in front of the temple; however, they did not uphold anything as pillars usually do. They were made of bronze, or one might say, copper. In effect, these pillars were strictly for ornamentation. They served no purpose otherwise. They did not hold up anything, did not support anything, and did not figure at all in the structure of the building. As stated, they were for ornamentation only.

THAT WHICH THE HOLY SPIRIT IS TELLING US

He is telling us several things:

- The names given the pillars simply mean "believers shall be established in the strength of the Lord."

- The pillars were for ornamentation only, meaning that believers are not actually needed in the kingdom of God, and that our presence is constituted as ornamentation.

- Copper is beautiful if it is regularly scrubbed and honed; however, it corrodes very easily. If believers are what we ought to be, the beauty will be apparent, otherwise, not so!

- Inasmuch as the temple faced the east, when the sun would rise each morning over Mount Olivet, it would strike those pillars first and create a beautiful light display. We must understand that as believers, our beauty is only in Christ. Otherwise, there is no beauty. We are merely, if we are at all, a reflection of His glory; at least, that's what we are supposed to be. This means we have no glory of our own; all is in Christ.

Fairest Lord Jesus,
Ruler of all nature,
Oh You of God and man the Son;
You will I cherish, You will I honor,
You my soul's glory, joy, and crown.

Fair are the meadows,
Fairer still the woodlands,
Robed in the blooming garb of spring;
Jesus is fairer, Jesus is purer,
Who makes the woeful heart to sing.

Fair is the sunshine,
Fairer still the moonlight,
And fair the twinkling starry host;
Jesus shines brighter, Jesus shines purer,
Than all the angels heaven can boast.

All fairest beauty,
Heavenly and earthly,
Wondrously, Jesus is found in Thee;
None can be nearer, fairer, or dearer,
Than You my Saviour are to me.

THE SPECIFICATIONS

THE SPECIFICATIONS

"*MOREOVER HE MADE AN* altar of brass (copper), *twenty cubits the length thereof* (30 feet), *and twenty cubits the breadth thereof, and ten cubits the height thereof. Also he made a molten sea of ten cubits* (15 feet) *from brim to brim, round in compass, and five cubits* (seven and a half feet) *the height thereof; and a line of thirty cubits did compass it round about. And under it was the similitude of oxen, which did compass it round about: ten in a cubit, compassing the sea round about. Two rows of oxen were cast, when it was cast. It stood upon twelve oxen, three looking toward the north, and three looking toward the west, and three looking toward the south, and three looking toward the east: and the sea was set above upon them, and all their hinder parts were inward. And the thickness of it was an handbreadth, and the brim of it like the work of the brim of a cup, with flowers of lilies; and it received and held three thousand baths*" (II Chron. 4:1-5).

DIMENSIONS AND MEANINGS

The dimensions given concerning the brazen altar were, as stated, the same dimensions as the most Holy Place. The altar portrayed God's judgment on sin. The Holy of Holies portrayed His mercy and grace; therefore, God's mercy and grace are as large as His judgment.

As it regards the *"twelve oxen"* of verse 4, the number 12 signifies God's government, while oxen symbolize the Word of God. So, God's government is built entirely upon His Word, from which we must not deviate at all.

The latter portion of verse 4 signifies that God's government is the same throughout the entirety of the earth. In other words, there is no such thing as a white man's gospel, a black man's gospel, etc. It is one gospel for the entirety of mankind, and for all time.

As it regards the oxen holding up the great laver, considering that the oxen represent the Word of God, this tells us the power of the Word.

Three thousand baths of verse 5 constitute approximately 18,000 gallons. I Kings 7:26 says *"two thousand baths."* There is no contradiction. The maximum amount of water that the molten sea would hold was 3,000 baths. The amount it generally held was 2,000 baths.

THE BRAZEN ALTAR

The brazen altar sat immediately in front of the temple. One might say, I think, that this altar constituted the core of all for which the temple stood. As well, I think one might say without fear of contradiction that it was the single most important vessel of the entirety of the temple structure. While every vessel, of course, served a distinct purpose—all pointing to Christ—still, everything was dependent upon what took place at the brazen altar, namely the sacrifices.

As most know, the brazen altar was a portrayal, a type if you will, of the Cross of Calvary and God's judgment upon sin. It was carried out in the form of the sacrifice of His only Son, whose life was given for our sins. As we continue to say, Christ is the source of all things from God, while the Cross is the means by which these things are given to us, and all is superintended by the Holy Spirit.

Even the Holy of Holies, which represented the great throne of God, where God actually dwelt between the mercy seat and the cherubim, in an obvious way, depended upon the brazen altar and what was there done.

The high priest, who alone could come into the Holy of Holies, and then only once a year on the great Day of Atonement, dared not come in without blood, which, of course, pertained to the sacrifice offered up on the brazen altar.

THE GOLDEN ALTAR

As well, the priests came into the Holy Place constantly, at least twice a day, at the time of the morning and evening sacrifices. They were to take coals of fire from the brazen altar, place those coals on the golden altar (the altar of incense), and then pour incense on that. This filled the Holy Place with a sweet smelling fragrance. All of this typified Christ in His intercessory work. This was a type, a shadow if you will, of that which makes possible our prayers, our petitions, our praise, and our worship. None could be accepted were it not for the intercessory work of Christ, of which the golden altar was a type. So, we must never forget that all of this was made possible by the Cross.

As well, we must ever understand that no sacrifice was to be made on the golden altar, with that being reserved for the brazen altar. To have offered up sacrifice on the golden altar would have been stating that what Jesus did at the Cross was not enough. Anyone thinking such is forfeiting his salvation.

THE BRAZEN LAVER

This apparatus, which had five smaller lavers on each side, held about 18,000 gallons of water. The huge laver was for the priests to wash when they went into the Holy Place. The smaller lavers were used to wash the parts of the sacrifices that were to be offered. It was all a type of the Word of God, and failure to comply with the demands of the washings could well bring about the penalty of death. It signified the cleansing by the Word of God, which is incumbent upon every believer.

The giant laver sat upon 12 oxen, all made of copper. Three of the oxen looked toward the north, three toward the west, three toward the south, and three toward the east. This signified that the Word of God, of which these oxen were a type, was the same in all places and in every direction, in other words, every point of the compass. It is the gospel for the entirety of mankind.

As it regards the whole of humanity, irrespective of class, culture, or race, the problem with all is sin. The solution to that problem, and there is only one solution, is the Cross of the Lord Jesus Christ. Around the top of the great brazen laver, and more than likely, the smaller ones, as well, was carved into the copper *"flowers of lilies."* This signified the righteousness of Christ, which was all made possible by the Word, for Jesus is the living Word (Jn. 1:1).

THE WORD OF GOD

The giant brazen laver was 15 feet from brim to brim, seven and a half feet high, and 45 feet all the way around. Incidentally, it was about four inches thick. It weighed anywhere from 15 to 20 tons. It's depth—seven and a half feet—would have taken approximately 18,000 gallons of water, and completely filled, it would have weighed about 75 tons.

The 10 small lavers were supposed to contain about 300 gallons of water each, which made each one weigh about two tons. Jewish writers say that the water was changed daily so it would always be fresh and pure for use in the ceremonial worship.

The entirety of the apparatus of the brazen laver was a type of the Word of God. As the priest would look into the water, he would see his reflection as in a mirror, likewise, when we read and study the Word of God, we see our reflection in the Word, proclaiming to us what we are. The oxen stood for the indestructibility, power, and strength of the Word of God.

THE CROSS

When Jesus came and went to the Cross, His life, living, and death satisfied every demand of the law, meaning that all of this we are studying came to an end. Why would one want the shadow when one could have the substance?

All of this was ever meant to be temporary. It was all meant to point to Christ, who would fulfill all the requirements when He came, which He did.

Please understand that as important as all of this was, still, none of it saved anyone. It didn't matter how zealous the priests were in carrying out all the demands of the law, or even how much they should have done this. Men have always been saved in the same way. Before the Cross, they were saved by looking forward to that which would ultimately come. Now that it is a fact, men are saved by looking back to that finished work. This means that the Cross of Christ stands at the apex of humanity with everything straining toward that finished work.

To make too much of the Cross is impossible. To make too little of the Cross is to invite spiritual disaster.

THE WASHING

"He made also ten lavers, and put five on the right hand, and five on the left, to wash in them: such things as they offered for the *burnt offering they washed in them; but the sea was for the priests to wash in"* (II Chron. 4:6).

These smaller vessels were used to wash the sacrifices before they were offered.

As we have stated, the priests had to wash both their hands and feet every time they went into the temple, with the giant laver being for that purpose.

If it is to be noticed, the law demanded a constant doing.

THE WASHING OF THE HANDS AND THE FEET

As it regards the brazen laver, the Scripture says, *"For Aaron and his sons shall wash their hands and their feet thereat: When they go into the tabernacle of the congregation, they shall wash with water, that they die not; or when they come near to the altar to minister, to burn offerings made by fire unto the* LORD*: So they shall wash their hands and their feet, that they die not: and it shall be a statute forever to them, even to him and to his seed throughout their generations"* (Ex. 30:19-21).

All of this meant that every time the priests went into the tabernacle (or the temple), they were to wash both their hands and their feet. When they offered up the sacrifices on the great altar, they were, as well, to wash their hands and their feet before it was carried out. This meant they were washing constantly *"that they die not."*

All of this meant, and we continue to speak of the washing, that everything was to be done according to the Word of God, of which the water was a type.

THE WASHING OF THE FEET

As it regards the last Passover, the Scripture says that Jesus,

After that He poured water into a basin (spiritually, it referred to the Holy Spirit, which would pour from Him like a river [Jn. 7:38-39]), *and began to wash the disciples' feet* (presenting the servant principle which we are to follow, but even more particularly, the cleansing guaranteed by the Holy Spirit concerning our daily walk, which comes about according to our faith in Christ and what He did for us at the Cross), *and to wipe them with the towel wherewith He was girded* (refers to the incarnation, which made possible His death on Calvary that atoned for all sin and made cleansing possible for the human race). *Then comes He to Simon Peter* (seems to indicate it was Peter to whom He first approached): *and Peter said unto Him, Lord, do You wash my feet?* ('The flesh' cannot understand spiritual realities; it is too backward or too forward, too courageous or too cowardly; it is incapable of ever being right, and it is impossible to improve, consequently, it must 'die.')

SIMON PETER

Jesus answered and said unto him, What I do you know not now; but you shall know hereafter (when Peter was filled with the Spirit, which he was on the Day of Pentecost). *Peter said unto Him, You shall never wash my feet* (the Greek text actually says,

'Not while eternity lasts'; Calvin said, 'With God, obedience is better than worship'). *Jesus answered Him, If I wash you not, you have no part with Me* (the statement as rendered by Christ speaks to the constant cleansing needed regarding our everyday walk before the Lord, which the washing of the feet [our walk], at least in part, represented). *Simon Peter said unto Him, Lord, not my feet only, but also my hands and my head* (Chrysostom said, 'In his deprecation he was vehement, and his yielding more vehement, but both came from his love').

JESUS

Jesus said to him, He who is washed needs not save to wash his feet (as stated, pertains to our daily walk before God, which means that the believer doesn't have to get saved over and over again; the 'head' refers to our salvation, meaning that we do not have to be repeatedly saved, while the 'hands' refer to our 'doing,' signifying that this doesn't need to be washed because Christ has already done what needs to be done; all of this is in the spiritual sense), *but is clean every whit* (refers to salvation and pertains to the precious blood of Jesus that cleanses from all sin; the infinite sacrifice needs no repetition) (Jn. 13:5-10) (The Expositor's Study Bible).

The priests of old had to constantly wash both their hands and their feet because the law could not save and neither could it cleanse. This means that not only did their walk at times become polluted, but their doing did as well.

Since the Cross, while our *walk* needs attending constantly, even as Jesus here portrayed, the *doing* doesn't have to be done anymore. It has already been done in Christ.

OUR WALK BEFORE GOD

The Holy Spirit through the Apostle Paul used the word *walk* constantly as it describes our everyday life and living, in other words, our walk before God and our fellowman (Rom. 8:1).

How is the believer to look at this constant need? Should there be foot washing services each week at church?

No!

What Jesus did was an example and was carried out to teach the disciples and you and me a lesson.

No matter how consecrated to the Lord, there is nothing that we can personally do, at least within our own capabilities, that will cleanse our walk. So, how do we walk correctly before the Lord and do so on a constant basis?

WALKING AFTER THE SPIRIT

The Holy Spirit through Paul said:

There is therefore now no condemnation (guilt) *to them which are in Christ Jesus* (refers back to Romans 6:3-5 and our being baptized into His death, which speaks of the crucifixion), *who walk not after the flesh* (depending on one's personal strength, education, motivation, and ability, or great religious efforts in order to overcome sin), *but after the Spirit* (the Holy Spirit works exclusively within the legal confines of the finished work of Christ; our faith in that finished work, i.e., the Cross, guarantees the help of the Holy Spirit, which guarantees victory) (Rom. 8:1) (The Expositor's Study Bible).

So, what does it mean to walk after the Spirit?

Unfortunately, most people think the explanation of this question is that we do spiritual things. In other words, we are faithful to attend church, faithful in our giving of our tithes to the work of the Lord, faithful in witnessing to souls, and faithful in our prayer life and Bible study.

While all of these things are very, very important, actually Christian disciplines, which should be a part of all Christian life and living, still, that's not what Paul was talking about.

Walking after the Spirit simply means that we place our faith exclusively in Christ and what Christ has done for us at the Cross, and we don't allow it to be moved elsewhere (Rom. 8:2-11).

THE HOLY SPIRIT AND THE CROSS

The Spirit of God works exclusively within the parameters of the finished work of Christ, i.e., the Cross. It is the Cross of Christ that gave and gives the Holy Spirit the legal right to do all that He does. That's the reason that it is referred to as "the law." Please understand that when Paul used that word in Romans 8:2, he wasn't speaking of the law of Moses, but rather a law that was devised by the Godhead sometime in eternity past.

In the modern Christian climate, Jesus Christ is held up, at least to some extent, but the Cross is all but ignored. Please understand that if the believer tries to separate Christ from the Cross, he is left with *"another Jesus"* (II Cor. 11:4). That's the reason that Paul also said, *"We preach Christ crucified"* (I Cor. 1:23).

He did not only say, *"We preach Christ,"* but rather, *"We preach Christ crucified."* In other words, he never separated Christ from the Cross, i.e., what Christ did for us at the Cross and the victories there won.

So, to walk after the Spirit is simply to place our faith exclusively in Christ and what Christ did for us at the Cross, which then gives the Holy Spirit latitude to work within our lives.

WALKING AFTER THE FLESH

What did Paul mean by walking after the flesh?

He was referring to the natural strength, power, motivation, intellect, education, talents, and ability of the individual. Within themselves, these things aren't necessarily wrong. However, it's impossible to please the Lord, in other words, to successfully live for God by human means, as dedicated as those human means may very well be. When we look to these particular means within ourselves, it doesn't matter how dedicated we might be, how consecrated we might be, how sincere we might be, or how much we load up the flesh with Scriptures, still, the Scripture bluntly says, *"They who are in the flesh cannot please God"* (Rom. 8:8).

In other words, within himself, the believer cannot develop righteousness and holiness within his life by his own ability, strength, machinations, talent, etc. It is impossible. These are works that the Holy Spirit alone can bring about in our lives, and he does so by us placing our faith exclusively in Christ and the Cross.

WHY ARE OUR PERSONAL EFFORTS INSUFFICIENT?

Paul answered that as well. He said:

And if Christ be in you (He is in you through the power and person of the Holy Spirit [Gal. 2:20]), *the body is dead because of sin* (means that the physical body has been rendered helpless because of the fall; consequently, the believer trying to overcome by willpower presents a fruitless task); *but the Spirit is life because of righteousness* (only the Holy Spirit can make us what we ought to be, which means we cannot do it ourselves; once again, He performs all that He does within the confines of the finished work of Christ) (Rom. 8:10) (The Expositor's Study Bible).

Looking totally to Christ and what He did for us at the Cross instead of looking to our own strength and ability is the great struggle facing every child of God. In fact, because of this great struggle, most of that given to us by the Apostle Paul, which was inspired by the Holy Spirit, deals with this very subject.

When we depend totally on Christ and the Cross, it gives the Holy Spirit latitude to work within our lives because the way He works is by the means of the Cross. And yet, we find so little preaching and teaching from the modern pulpit regarding this which is so very, very important.

THE CRITERION FOR DISCIPLESHIP

Jesus bluntly and plainly told us,

If any man will come after Me (which is the criterion for discipleship), *let him deny himself* (not asceticism as many think, but rather that one denies one's own willpower, self-will, strength, and ability, depending totally on Christ), *and take up his cross* (the benefits of the Cross), *daily* (this is so important, our looking to the Cross, that we must renew our faith in what Christ has done for us even on a daily basis, for Satan will ever try to move us away from the Cross as the object of our faith, which always spells disaster), *and follow Me* (Christ can be followed only by the believer looking to the Cross and understanding what it accomplished, and by that means alone [Rom. 6:1-14; 8:1-11; I Cor. 1:17-18, 21, 23; 2:2; Gal. 6:14; Eph. 2:13-18; Col. 2:10-15]) (Lk. 9:23) (The Expositor's Study Bible).

DISCIPLE

The Lord then followed up by saying,

And whosoever does not bear his cross (this doesn't speak of suffering as most think, but rather ever making the Cross of Christ the object of our faith; we are saved and we are victorious not by suffering, although that sometimes will happen, or any other similar things, but rather by our faith, but always with the Cross of Christ as the object of that faith), *and come after Me* (one can follow Christ only by faith in what He has done for us at the Cross; He recognizes nothing else), *cannot be My disciple* (the statement as given by Christ is emphatic; if it's not faith in the Cross of Christ, then it's faith that God will not recognize, which means that such people are refused (Lk. 14:27) (The Expositor's Study Bible).

The Word of God must always be the criterion.

The Word of God, i.e., the Bible, is the single most important thing in the world. I know that's quite a statement, but it is true.

The second most important thing is that the believer understand what is said in the Word. Admittedly, some parts in the Bible, especially some of the prophecies given in the Old Testament, and even some of the teachings of Paul, are not easy to understand; therefore, every believer ought to set themselves to study the Word. They should ask the Lord to help them understand the Word; in effect, they should make it a lifelong project. It will be the most rewarding and the most fruitful thing in which anyone could ever begin to engage. As well, every believer should avail themselves of the opportunity of getting material that will help them understand the Word to a greater degree. That's what the Holy Spirit was meaning when He said through Paul:

> *And He gave some, apostles; and some, prophets; and some, evangelists; and some, pastors and teachers; For the perfecting of the saints, for the work of the ministry, for the edifying of the body of Christ: Till we all come in the unity of the faith, and of the knowledge of the Son of God, unto a perfect man, unto the measure of the stature of the fullness of Christ:*

And then he said,

> *That we henceforth be no more children, tossed to and fro, and carried about with every wind of doctrine, by the sleight of men, and cunning craftiness, whereby they lie in wait to deceive* (Eph. 4:11-14).

THE ATTACKS OF SATAN

Presently, Satan is attacking the Word of God maybe as never before; however, He is doing it in a very subtle way.

When I was just a boy, Satan, of course, made his efforts at that time as well. However, in those days, it usually was a frontal attack against the Bible, which was mostly generated by the so-called modernists. Today, scores of versions of the Bible are being brought out, such as the *Message Bible* for instance. Actually, such is really not a Bible, but rather a collection of religious ideas.

Please understand that unless your Bible is a word-for-word translation, then you really do not have a Bible but only a religious book. The *Message Bible*, plus scores of others like that particular version, is really not a Bible. It is Satan's way of diluting, perverting, and ultimately destroying the Word of God.

WHAT IS A WORD-FOR-WORD TRANSLATION?

The term "word-for-word translation" simply means that the translators did their very best to translate from the original Hebrew and Greek text into the language at hand, in this case, English.

There are no original manuscripts of the Bible left. However, there are thousands of copies that do remain, with some of them going back to within 300 years of the original. The Dead Sea scrolls are a case in point, although they were about 800 years from the original manuscript. The Old Testament was originally written in Hebrew, with the New Testament originally written in Greek. Not having printing presses in those days, scribes were used to make copies of the original manuscript, and there were, as stated, thousands made.

We believe that the Lord inspired the writers in that they wrote exactly what He wanted and desired, meaning that every word in the Bible is important.

WHAT IS INSPIRATION?

Inspiration simply means, at least in this case, that the Lord gave to the writers that which He wanted, and consequently, it is error-free. This means there are no contradictions, and it's all because it is the Word of God.

The details of inspiration mean that the Lord searched through the vocabulary of every writer and, thereby, chose the exact words that He wanted as it regarded what was being said.

These men knew what they were writing. They did not go into a trance as some teach, but rather wrote as the Holy Spirit gave them the very words they were to use. It would be somewhat like a computer searching for particular words as the Lord searched through their vocabulary and then had them to write what He so desired. That's the reason Jesus said, *"Man shall not live by bread alone, but by every Word that proceeds out of the mouth of God"* (Mat. 4:4).

THE KING JAMES VERSION

This is what makes it so wrong for people to change the words given by the Holy Spirit and, thereby, substitute their own words to take their place. However, there is something else that needs to be said about that.

I use the King James Version of the Bible, believing that it is still the very best version that's in the world today, at least as it regards English.

However, the reader must understand that the King James Version has been edited two or three times. I have a copy of one of the pages of one of the original King James Versions. The Elizabethan English at that time was so different from what we now speak that it's very difficult to even read what was printed.

So, the King James Version has been edited two or three times because of the change of language, and rightly so.

This doesn't mean that the words were changed, but that the Elizabethan English was changed to more accommodating English for the present time, and, as stated, rightly so.

For instance, there are still some words in the modern King James Version that are antiquated, meaning that we do not use them anymore. These are words such as *"hast,"* etc. Consequently, when the Lord helped us to put together The Expositor's Study Bible, we changed some of those words to modern English—words which mean the same thing but are more familiar with present day understanding.

The reader must understand that when the original writers wrote the text (we speak of Moses, David, Isaiah, Peter, Paul, John, etc.), they didn't use Elizabethan English. So, the idea is, a word-for-word translation must be just that, meaning that the translators have done everything within their power to bring the original Hebrew and Greek text over into the language at hand. As already stated, in this case, it would be English.

THE BIBLE

The Bible is the road map for eternity and the blueprint for life. There is no other. There are many other books that claim to be holy, but they aren't. The Bible alone fits that standard. It is the Word of God, and there is only one Word of God.

I have said many times, and continue to say, personally, I only have one desire, and that is to understand the Word of God, whatever it teaches. I have no personal preference regarding what the Bible teaches. I just want to know what it does teach, and prayerfully, understand it correctly and deliver it to the public.

THE SACRED VESSELS

"And he made ten candlesticks of gold according to their form, and set them in the temple, five on the right hand, and five on the left. He made also ten tables, and placed them in the temple, five on the right side, and five on the left. And he made an hundred basins of gold" (II Chron. 4:7-8).

The word *candlesticks* should have been translated lampstands.

The lampstands typify the fact that Christ is the light of the world.

The "ten tables" were tables that held shewbread.

There was only one lampstand and one table in the tabernacle, but here there are 10 of each.

The tables each held 12 loaves of bread, which had to be eaten by the priests every Sabbath, with new loaves taking their place. The bread was a type of Christ as the *"Bread of Life"* (Jn. 6:48).

THE LAMPSTANDS

These lampstands provided light for the Holy Place in order that the priests could carry out their work. They were types of Christ, as stated, as the light of the world.

Every morning at 9 a.m. and every afternoon at 3 p.m., the priests were to trim the wicks on each lamp in order that soot would not develop, thereby, polluting the Holy Place. As well, the oil was to be replenished at that time also.

The lampstands, in a sense, typified the Lord Jesus Christ, the Holy Spirit, and believers.

The golden part of the stand—all of it of pure gold—typified Christ in His deity.

The oil typified the Holy Spirit, as would be obvious, and the wicks that had to be trimmed twice a day typified believers. That was the only part of the lampstand that could be polluted and, thereby, not burn brightly as it should. Therefore, it typified believers. As believers, we constantly need trimming in order that we function as we should function. How many believers are burning brightly, and how many believers are smoking up the Holy Place?

BELIEVERS IN CHRIST

The three prongs on each side of the main stem (totaling six), as it regards the lampstand, were, in a sense, also types of believers. Six is the number of man, while seven is the number of God. Christ is the main stem, as would be obvious. Believers are "in Christ" exactly as the three stems from each side were in the main stem. However, here is the thing about the joining of the side stems with the main stem:

These stems were not welded to the main stem or fixed in any manner. When the goldsmith fashioned the lampstand, he fashioned it, as stated, out of one piece of gold. Consequently, each stem was a part of the main stem exactly as a limb is the part of a tree.

This portrays the fact that we, as believers, are more than merely being attached to Christ, inasmuch as we are "in Christ." Jesus said:

"At that day you shall know that I am in My Father, and you in Me, and I in you" (Jn. 14:20).

As well, Paul used the term *"in Christ Jesus,"* or one of its derivatives, such as *"in Him,"* over a hundred times in his 14 epistles.

We are "in Christ" by virtue of His atoning death on the Cross and our acceptance of Him as our Saviour and Lord.

THE SCRIPTURE SAYS ...

Know you not, that so many of us as were baptized into Jesus Christ (plainly says that this baptism is into Christ and not water [I Cor. 1:17; 12:13; Gal. 3:28-29; Eph. 4:5; Col. 2:10-15]) *were baptized into His death?* (When Christ died on the Cross, in the mind of God, we died with Him; in other words, He became our substitute, and our identification with Him in His death gives us all the benefits for which He died; the idea is that He did it all for us!) *Therefore we are buried with Him by baptism into death* (not only did we die with Him, but we were buried with Him, as well, which means that all the sin and transgression of the past were buried; when they put Him in the tomb, they put all of our sins into that tomb as well): *that like as Christ was raised up from the dead by the glory of the Father, even so we also should walk in newness of life* (we died with Him, we were buried with Him, and His resurrection was our resurrection to a 'newness of life'). *For if we have been planted together* (with Christ) *in the likeness of His death* (Paul proclaims the Cross as the instrument through which all blessings come; consequently, the Cross must ever be the object of our faith, which gives the Holy Spirit latitude to work within our lives), *we shall be also in the likeness of His resurrection* (we can have the 'likeness of His resurrection,' i.e., live this resurrection life, only as long as we understand the 'likeness of His death,' which refers to the Cross as the means by which all of this is done) (Rom. 6:3-5) (The Expositor's Study Bible).

IS IT POSSIBLE FOR THE BELIEVER TO BE TAKEN OUT OF CHRIST?

The word *believer* proclaims the fact that the individual has faith in Christ and what Christ has done for us at the Cross. As such, no, the believer cannot be removed from Christ.

It is faith that gets the believer into Christ, which refers to faith in Christ and what He did at the Cross. Even though the believing sinner may understand little of Christ when he first comes to the Lord, still, it is his faith that makes all of this possible. Of course, his faith is supplied by the Holy Spirit, and that is tendered upon the Word of God that's been delivered to the believing sinner in some way. The Holy Spirit supplies the faith, and the believing sinner then believes, at least if he does. At that moment, he is saved.

So, faith gets one in (Rom. 5:1-2), and it is faith that keeps one in (Rom. 6:1-14). However, if the believer ceases to believe, thereby, ceasing to be a believer, then such a person is reverted to the category of being lost.

LISTEN TO PAUL

For it is impossible for those who were once enlightened (refers to those who have accepted the light of the Gospel, which means accepting Christ and His great sacrifice), *and have tasted of the heavenly gift* (pertains to Christ and what He did at the Cross), *and were made partakers of the Holy Spirit* (which takes place when a person comes to Christ), *And have tasted the good Word of God* (is not language that is used of an impenitent sinner, as some claim; the unsaved have no relish whatsoever for the truth of God and see no beauty in it), *and the powers of the world to come* (pertains to the work of the Holy Spirit within hearts and lives, which the unsaved cannot have or know), *If they shall fall away* (should have been translated, 'and having fallen away'), *to renew them again unto repentance* ('again' states they had once repented but have now turned their backs on Christ); *seeing they crucify to themselves the Son of God afresh* (means they no longer believe what Christ did at the Cross, actually concluding Him to be an imposter; the only way any person can truly repent is to place his faith in Christ and the Cross;

if that is denied, there is no repentance), *and put Him to an open shame* (means such a person holds Christ up to public ridicule; Paul wrote this epistle because some Christian Jews were going back into Judaism, or seriously contemplating doing so) (Heb. 6:4-6) (The Expositor's Study Bible).

IN CHRIST

Christ and what He did at the Cross is the only way a person can be saved, and continued faith in that sacrifice is the only thing that keeps us *"in Christ."* With that being lost, which means that a person of his own freewill makes a conscious decision to cease to believe, then that individual is lost. As stated, it's faith that got us in, and it's faith that keeps us in. As long as faith is maintained in Christ and what He did at the Cross, salvation is maintained, as well, irrespective of the state of the individual otherwise.

WHAT DO WE MEAN BY THE TERM "FAITH"?

Always and without exception, when the word *faith* is used in the Bible, at least as it refers to the individual and the Lord, it is referring to faith in Christ and what He did for us at the Cross. In other words, the Cross of Christ must always be the object of our faith.

The truth is, every person in the world has faith, but it is only faith in Christ and the Cross that is recognized by the Lord. To merely have faith is not enough. It must be faith in Christ and the Cross, meaning that the Cross of Christ, as stated, is the object of one's faith, and is always the object of one's faith. Paul said:

> *Therefore being justified by faith* (this is the only way one can be justified; refers to faith in Christ and what He did at the Cross [I Cor. 1:17-18, 23; 2:2), *we have peace with God* (justifying peace) *through our Lord Jesus Christ* (what He did at the Cross): *By Whom also we have access by faith into this grace* (we have access to the goodness of God by faith in Christ) *wherein we stand* (wherein alone we can stand), *and rejoice in hope* (a hope that is guaranteed) *of the glory of God* (our faith in Christ always brings glory to God; anything else brings glory to self, which God can never accept) (Rom. 5:1-2) (The Expositor's Study Bible).

CHRIST AND THE CROSS

Christ is to never be separated from the Cross, and by that, we are not referring to the wooden beam, but rather to what He there did.

At the Cross, which refers to His atoning death—the sacrifice of Himself—He atoned for all sin, past, present, and future, at least for all who will believe. In the atoning for all sin, this removed the legal right that Satan had to hold man in bondage. Sin was that which gave him that right, and with all sin atoned—taken away—that legal right the Evil One had has now been removed. So, if Satan is able to hold a believer in bondage, it is because the believer has placed his faith in something else other than Christ and the Cross. This gives Satan the consent to place such a one in bondage. That's why Paul also said:

"Stand fast therefore in the liberty wherewith Christ has made us free (we were made free and refers to freedom to live a holy life by evidencing faith in Christ and the Cross), *and be not entangled again with the yoke of bondage.* (To abandon the Cross and go under law of any kind guarantees bondage once again to the sin nature.)" (Gal. 5:1) (The Expositor's Study Bible).

JESUS CHRIST IS THE SAVIOUR

The modern church is big to laud Christ—most of the time as a miracle worker, a great example, a great teacher, etc.—while conveniently forgetting that while He definitely was all of these things, most of all, however, He is Saviour.

That's what He came to this world to do—to free man from the bondage of sin. He did it by the Cross, a plan of redemption, which, in essence, was formulated in the mind of the Godhead from before the foundation of the world (I Pet. 1:18-20).

So, when the believer thinks "Christ," it always must be in conjunction with His sacrificial atoning death on the Cross of Calvary. That's the reason that Paul said, *"We preach Christ crucified"* (I Cor. 1:23).

That's the reason the great apostle also said, *"Christ sent me not to baptize, but to preach the Gospel: not with wisdom of words, lest the Cross of Christ should be made of none effect"* (I Cor. 1:17).

That's the reason that he also stated, *"For I determined not to know anything among you, save Jesus Christ, and Him crucified"* (I Cor. 2:2).

Paul never separated Christ from the Cross because, while Jesus was most definitely the source of all things that we receive from God, it was the Cross that provided the means for these things to be done. We must never forget that!

TABLES OF SHEWBREAD

Everything in the tabernacle and everything in the temple that would be built portrayed Christ in some way. It pictured who He was, what He would do, and how He would do it, which is what makes the Old Testament so important. Anything that pertains to Christ is of utmost significance, as should be obvious.

The tables of shewbread pictured Christ as the Bread of Life. In fact, He mentioned this in John 6:35. He said:

"I am the Bread of Life (proclaims Him dropping all disguise and gathering up into one burning Word all the previous teaching which they might have fathomed but did not)*: he who comes to Me shall never hunger* (pertains to spiritual hunger)*; and he who believes on Me shall never thirst* (pertains to spiritual thirst; Christ satisfies all spiritual desire) (The Expositor's Study Bible).

Our Lord then said: *"I am the living bread which came down from heaven* (now proclaims Jesus presenting Himself as God ['I am'], while in the previous verse, He presented Himself as man; and so He is the God-man Jesus Christ)*: if any man eat* *of this bread, he shall live forever* (says the same thing as in the previous verse but in a different way; there He said, 'And not die,' now He says, 'Shall live forever'; the latter adds to the former): *and the bread that I will give is My flesh, which I will give for the life of the world* (this speaks of Him giving Himself on the Cross as a sacrifice, which would guarantee salvation for all who would believe)" (Jn. 6:51) (The Expositor's Study Bible).

EATING THE BREAD

On the Sabbath, the priests had to eat all of the loaves of bread on the 10 tables. Counting 12 loaves to the table, there would have been 120 loaves. These were replaced by fresh loaves.

The eating of the bread, in essence, portrayed the taking of Christ, and doing so by placing faith in Him and what He did at the Cross.

When the believing sinner accepts Christ, in the mind of God, that believing sinner is actually placed into Christ, which includes His death, His burial, and His resurrection (Rom. 6:3-5).

Jesus was and is the last Adam and the second man (I Cor. 15:45-47), and as such, He is our substitute, "our representative man."

Being *in Christ* means that whatever He is, we are that as well. In fact, everything He did was done in totality for us. He did nothing for heaven, for angels, for God the Father, or for Himself, but rather, it was all done for us, i.e., for sinners.

Did the priests understand this symbolism in their eating the bread? It is doubtful! Quite possibly, some few did, but more than likely, that number was small.

To prove my point, Israel came to believe that engaging in the ritual, i.e., the ceremony, granted them some type of dispensation with God. They even finally came to the place that they believed in a nationalistic salvation, hence, being a Jew was sufficient enough, unless some of their rules were broken. That's why John the Baptist said when he came, *"And think not to say within yourselves, We have Abraham to our father: for I say unto you, that God is able of these stones to raise up children unto Abraham"* (Mat. 3:9).

THE BRAZEN LAVER

"Furthermore he made the court of the priests, and the great court, and doors for the court, and overlaid the doors of them with brass. And he set the sea on the right side of the east end, over against the south" (II Chron. 4:9-10).

- The doors also typified Christ; He said *"I am the door"* (Jn. 10:9).

- The brass signified the humanity of Christ.

- The brazen laver, i.e., the sea, had its position as the tabernacle laver of old, which was between the altar and the porch.

THE COURTS

As is obvious, very little information is given here as it regards the courts proper. The emphasis seems to be on the material used, such as the doors covered with copper.

Actually, there were three courts in front of the temple. The first one was nearest the temple and was referred to as the *"court of men"* or *"the court of Israel."* This means that only men and, of course, priests could go into that court.

The court immediately behind the court of Israel was the *"court of women."*

The last court was the *"court of Gentiles,"* which was separated from the court of women by a barrier. The height of the barrier was not given, but it is believed that it was about four feet high. For Gentiles to cross that barrier, they could be stoned to death.

The women were placed in a secondary position, as is obvious, because of Eve who failed the Lord first of all.

GENTILES

As it regarded the Gentiles, they had no covenant with the Lord whatsoever; however, if they so chose, Gentiles could become proselyte Jews, which some did. To be saved, this would have to be their course of action.

When Jesus came, all of this was addressed. Paul said:

> *Wherefore remember, that you being in time past Gentiles in the flesh, who are called uncircumcision* (referred to the Gentiles

not being in covenant with God; physical circumcision under the old economy was its external sign) *by that which is called the circumcision in the flesh made by hands* (is said by Paul in this manner, regarding the Jews, in contradistinction from the circumcision of the heart)*; That at that time you were without Christ* (describes the former condition of the Gentiles, who had no connection with Christ before the Cross)*, being aliens from the commonwealth of Israel, and strangers from the covenants of promise, having no hope, and without God in the world* (all of this argues a darkened and perverted heart; the Gentiles had no knowledge of God at that time)*:*

IN CHRIST

But now in Christ Jesus (proclaims the basis of all salvation) *you who sometimes* (times past) *were far off* (far from salvation) *are made nigh* (near) *by the blood of Christ.* (The sacrificial atoning death of Jesus Christ transformed the relations of God with mankind. In Christ, God reconciled not a nation, but 'a world' to Himself [II Cor. 5:19].) *For He* (Christ) *is our peace* (through Christ and what He did at the Cross, we have peace with God)*, who has made both one* (Jews and Gentiles)*, and has broken down the middle wall of partition between us* (between Jews and Gentiles. All come the same way, by Christ)*; Having abolished in His flesh* (speaking of His death on the Cross, by which He redeemed humanity, which also means He didn't die spiritually, as some claim) *the enmity* (the hatred between God and man, caused by sin), *even the law of commandments contained in ordinances* (pertains to the law of Moses, and more particularly, the Ten Commandments); *for to make in Himself of twain* (of Jews and Gentiles) *one new man, so making peace* (which again was accomplished by the Cross); *And that He* (Christ) *might reconcile both* (Jews and Gentiles) *unto God in one body* (the church) *by the Cross* (it is by the atonement only that men ever become reconciled to God), *having slain the enmity thereby* (removed the barrier between God and sinful man): *And came and preached peace to you which were afar off* (proclaims the Gospel going to the Gentiles), *and to them who were nigh.* (This refers to the Jews. It is the same message for both).

ACCESS

For through Him (through Christ) *we both* (Jews and Gentiles) *have access by one Spirit unto the Father.* (If the sinner comes by the Cross, the Holy Spirit opens the door, otherwise, it is barred [Jn. 10:1].) *Now* (speaks of the present state of believers) *therefore you are no more strangers and foreigners* (pertains to what Gentiles once were), *but fellowcitizens with the saints* (speaks of Gentiles now having access the same as Jews, all due to the Cross), *and of the household of God* (a progressive relationship with God in Christ); *And are built upon the foundation* (the Cross) *of the apostles and prophets* (apostles serve as leadership under the new covenant, with prophets having served in that capacity under the old), *Jesus Christ Himself being the chief corner stone* (presents the part of the foundation which holds everything together; Jesus Christ is the 'chief corner stone' by virtue of what He did at the Cross) (Eph. 2:11-20) (The Expositor's Study Bible).

Now, all are one in Christ, whether Jew or Gentile, or whether male or female, irrespective of race or color. As someone has said, "The ground is level at the foot of the Cross."

THE THRONE OF GRACE

Thank God that Jesus opened the door that whosoever will may come and take of the Water of Life freely (Rev. 22:17).

Now, due to Christ and what He did at the Cross, there are no longer various or different courts. In the spiritual sense, there is still a Holy of Holies, and thank God.

Paul also wrote concerning that. He said:

"Let us therefore come boldly unto the throne of grace (presents the seat of divine power, and yet the source of boundless grace), *that we may obtain mercy* (presents that which we want first), *and find grace to help in time of need* (refers to the goodness of God extended to all who come, and during any 'time of need'; all made possible by the Cross)" (Heb. 4:16) (The Expositor's Study Bible).

This means that every believer, irrespective as to whom he might be, has access to the very throne of God and can come to that throne any time, providing he does so in the name of Jesus.

GOLD

And Huram made the pots, and the shovels, and the basins. And Huram finished the work that he was to make for King Solomon for the house of God; To wit, the two pillars, and the pommels, and the chapiters which were on the top of the two pillars, and the two wreaths to cover the two pommels of the chapiters which were on the top of the pillars; And four hundred pomegranates on the two wreaths; two rows of pomegranates on each wreath, to cover the two pommels of the chapiters which were upon the pillars. He made also bases, and lavers made he upon the bases; One sea, and twelve oxen under it. The pots also, and the shovels, and the fleshhooks, and all their instruments, did Huram his father make to King Solomon for the house of the LORD *of bright brass. In the plain of Jordan did the king cast them, in the clay ground between Succoth and Zeredathah. Thus Solomon made all these vessels in great abundance: for the weight of the brass could not be found out. And Solomon made all the vessels that were for the house of God, the golden altar also, and the tables whereon the shewbread was set; More-over the candlesticks (lampstands) with their lamps, that they should burn after the manner before the oracle, of pure gold; And the flowers, and the lamps, and the tongs, made he of gold, and that perfect gold; And the snuffers, and the basins, and the spoons, and the censers, of pure gold: and the entry of the house, the inner doors thereof for the most Holy Place, and the doors of the house of the temple, were of gold* (II Chron. 4:11-22) (The Expositor's Study Bible).

DEATH AND RESURRECTION

In a very limited sense, Hiram may be said to be a type of the Holy Spirit, who will finish the work regarding the church. Therefore, He will present us faultless before the throne of God (Jude 1:24). The *"pomegranates"* were typical of the fruit of the Spirit. The *"chains,"* or *"wreaths,"* typified our union with Christ.

Verse 17 represents death and resurrection. In a sense, there must be a death to the old self, with the new self raised in the identification of Christ. This means that all former identity for the believer must be lost. What we were before salvation is of no consequence. Truly, the Holy Spirit is making a *new creation,* which can only be carried out by our understanding that we are baptized into His death, buried with Him by baptism into death, and raised with Him in newness of life (Rom. 6:3-4). So, all of these heathen golden idols, along with the silver and the brass, had to be melted—which means they lost their old identity—and then fashioned into a new mold in order to be of fit use for the temple.

This is a picture of what the Spirit of God does with us, which is carried out by and through the Cross (I Cor. 1:17-18, 23; 2:2).

The *"golden altar"* of verse 19 actually was the altar of incense, which stood immediately in front of the Holy of Holies.

The *"pure gold,"* actually all the gold that was used in the temple to whatever degree, typified the deity of Christ. The term *"pure gold"* meant that it contained no alloy whatsoever.

There is no way into this *"house of God"* except through the Lord Jesus Christ, who is the *"door"* (Jn. 10:9).

THE BRASS, GOLD, AND SILVER

All of this abundance of brass, gold, and silver, which was taken from the heathen in battles fought by David, would now be used for the temple. No doubt, the brass, gold, and silver had been used to a great degree in all types of vessels as it regarded idol worship. There were, no doubt, altars to idols made of gold, with silver and brass used in this capacity as well. There would have been doors made of this material in these heathen temples, as well as altars, altar rails, and actually, idols themselves. They had all been taken by David, carried to Jerusalem, and there deposited in warehouses to await the construction of the temple.

All of this is a perfect example of what we were before coming to Christ. Let it be understood that it really doesn't matter what the person was before conversion. Whatever he was, whatever type of talent he had, or whatever it was that made him great in the world, it holds no weight with the Lord whatsoever. In fact, every vestige of the world has to be eradicated, and there is only one way it can be done.

PREVIOUS IDENTITY MUST BE LOST

At a point in time when the temple was under construction, all of these heathen altar rails, golden doors, or whatever they may have been, were taken to the plain of Jordan. Now, the real work of the Spirit would begin.

According to verse 17, all of the gold and whatever it represented was put in one pile, with the silver in another and the brass in another. In succession, it was all placed into a furnace and melted. In other words, all identity with what it was before was now being erased.

No matter how beautiful it may have been in a heathen temple, all of that had to be eliminated. The fire of the furnace would attend to that. The molten material would then be poured into molds designed for the use of the temple.

THE WORK OF THE SPIRIT WITHIN OUR LIVES

It is not an easy thing, a simple thing, or a quick thing for the Holy Spirit to bring us to the place He desires that we be.

The believer must learn to walk after the Spirit instead of walking after the flesh. It is not nearly as simple as it sounds.

Simon Peter addressed this when he said: *"Beloved, think it not strange concerning the fiery trial which is to try you* (trials do not merely happen; they are designed by wisdom and operated by love; Job proved this), *as though some strange thing happened unto you* (your trial, whatever it is, is not unique; many others are experiencing the same thing!)*"* (I Pet. 4:12).

We as believers do not give up works of the flesh easily, especially considering that most of them are so very religious. These are *our works,* and as such, we are proud of them and part with them very reluctantly.

Abraham is an excellent example.

He and Sarah attempted to help God bring about the promise. The result was Ishmael, a work of the flesh. Ultimately, Isaac was born, who was a work of the Holy Spirit in every capacity;

however, the effect of the birth of Isaac was to make manifest the character of Ishmael. Ishmael hated him, and so did his mother. Prompted by her, he sought to murder Isaac (Gal. 4:29), and with his mother, he was justly expelled. Both merited a more severe sentence. Thus, the birth of Isaac, which filled Sarah's heart with mirth, filled Hagar's with murder.

THE NEW AND THE OLD NATURE
IN THE BELIEVER

Isaac and Ishmael symbolized the new and the old nature in the believer. Sarah and Hagar typified the two covenants of works and grace, of bondage and liberty (Gal., Chpt. 4). The birth of the new nature demands the expulsion of the old. It is impossible to improve the old. The Holy Spirit says in Romans, Chapter 8, verse 7, that it *"is enmity against God: for it is not subject to the law of God, neither indeed can be."* If it cannot be subject to the law of God, how can it be improved? How foolish, therefore, appears the doctrine of moral evolution!

The divine way of holiness is to put off the old man just as Abraham put off Ishmael. Man's way of holiness is to improve the old man, that is, to improve Ishmael. The effort is both foolish and hopeless. Of course, the casting out of Ishmael was *"very grievous in Abraham's sight"* (Gen. 21:11) because it always causes a struggle to cast out this element of bondage, that is, salvation or sanctification by works, for legalism is dear to the heart. Ishmael was the fruit, and to Abraham, the fair fruit of his own energy and planning. However, Ishmael had to go, and, likewise, the flesh in our hearts and lives has to go as well.

(The material regarding Abraham was derived from the work of George Williams.)

THE EXAMPLE GIVEN BY OUR LORD

The Scripture says, *"And He commanded the multitude to sit down on the grass, and took the five loaves, and the two fishes, and looking up to heaven, He blessed, and brake, and gave the loaves to His disciples, and the disciples to the multitude"* (Mat. 14:19).

Please notice the order:

- He took
- He blessed
- He broke
- He gave.

If it is to be noticed, when a person comes to Christ, generally, great blessings follow, but we find that it does not stop there.

Then comes the *breaking.* It's not pleasant, which means it's certainly not enjoyable; however, it is so very, very necessary. Only after one has been *broken* can one then be *given* to the world.

We have far too many Christians who are trying to give themselves to the cause of Christ without being properly broken. The only thing that can be given in such a circumstance is *self,* which cannot help anyone.

It's difficult for us to realize that after we are born again and Spirit-filled, still, there is a lot of work for the Spirit to do within our hearts and lives in order to bring us to the place we ought to be. In fact, and I think one can say without fear of contradiction, the breaking is something that is a life-long project. Once we think the breaking has achieved its purpose, we then find that there are other areas of *the flesh* that need to be addressed.

THE CLOSER WE GET TO THE LORD

I recently mentioned to our congregation at Family Worship Center that the closer we get to the Lord, the more we see how wonderful the Lord is, but at the same time, we see how lacking that we actually are. In fact, the closer we get to the Lord, the more the light shines upon us and reveals the flaws, which may have been somewhat hidden otherwise. Make no mistake about it, every one of us is riddled with flaws, which the Holy Spirit alone can address.

That's the reason Jesus said that if we are to come after Him, we must deny ourselves and take up the Cross daily and follow Him (Lk. 9:23). In fact, till the believer properly understands the Cross, or at least has a modicum of understanding regarding this great work, there is no way the flesh can be subdued within our lives. The Holy Spirit works entirely within the framework of the Cross of Christ. He doesn't demand much of us, but He does demand that our faith be implicitly, and even explicitly, in the Cross of Christ (Gal., Chpt. 5; 6:14).

A wonderful Saviour is Jesus my Lord,
A wonderful Saviour to me;
He hides my soul in the cleft of the rock,
Where rivers of pleasure I see.

A wonderful Saviour is Jesus my Lord,
He takes my burden away;
He holds me up, and I shall not be moved,
He gives me strength as my day.

With numberless blessings, each moment He crowns,
And filled with His fullness divine,
I sing in my rapture, O glory to God,
For such a Redeemer as mine!

When clothed in His brightness, transported I rise,
To meet Him in clouds of the sky,
His perfect salvation, His wonderful love,
I'll shout with the millions on high.

THE DEDICATION OF
THE TEMPLE

CHAPTER TEN
THE DEDICATION
OF THE TEMPLE

"THUS ALL THE WORK that Solomon made for the house of
the LORD was finished: and Solomon brought in all the things that
David his father had dedicated; and the silver, and the gold, and
all the instruments, put he among the treasures of the house of God"
(II Chron. 5:1).

THE WORK IS FINISHED

Solomon was seven years in building the temple (I Ki. 6:38).
Now it was time for the dedication.

All of the sacred vessels that had been in the tabernacle, such
as the altar of incense, the golden lampstand, etc., were now
brought to the temple and "put among the treasures of the house
of God." The dedication of the temple was approximately a year
after it was finished.

The Lord would dwell in this house, actually in the Holy of Holies between the mercy seat and the cherubim. It would be His only abiding place on earth; consequently, Israel was blessed indeed! No other nation in the world had the privilege of Jehovah being in their midst.

Today, due to what Christ has done at the Cross, the Holy Spirit, who once occupied that house of so long ago, now occupies our physical bodies. Paul said:

"Know you not that you are the temple of God (where the Holy Spirit abides)*, and that the Spirit of God dwells in you?* (That makes the born-again believer His permanent home)*"* (I Cor. 3:16) (The Expositor's Study Bible).

THE HOLY SPIRIT

Let us state it again:

This wonderful privilege of having the Holy Spirit abide with us permanently (Jn. 14:16) came about at great price—a price paid by our Redeemer, the Lord Jesus Christ. It took the offering of Himself in sacrifice, which He did on the Cross, to satisfy the terrible penalty of sin that was leveled at all of humanity. His sacrifice paid the price for all who will believe (Jn. 3:16).

The Holy Spirit is God. He is, as one might say, the third person of the triune Godhead of *"God the Father, God the Son, and God the Holy Spirit."*

He occupies this physical frame and even our souls and spirits, at least for those who are born again, in order to carry out a particular work in our lives. At least a part of that work is:

- The Holy Spirit reproves of sin and of righteousness and of judgment (Jn. 16:8). In other words, it is the business of the Holy Spirit to rid us of all sin. This does not mean sinless perfection because the Bible does not teach such, but it does mean that the sin nature is to no longer have dominion over us (Rom. 6:14). Ridding us of all sin can be done only by the believer placing His faith exclusively in Christ and the Cross.

- He is to guide us into all truth (Jn. 16:13).

- He is to show us things to come (Jn. 16:13).

- He is to glorify Christ within our hearts and lives (Jn. 16:14).

- He is to show us all things for which Christ has paid such a price (Jn. 16:14).

- He is to give us power to carry out the work of God (Acts 1:8).

- He quickens our mortal bodies that we might be able to live for God as we should live, which He alone can do (Rom. 8:11).

- We have access by the Holy Spirit unto the Father (Eph. 2:18).

THE FEAST OF TABERNACLES

"Then Solomon assembled the elders of Israel, and all the heads of the tribes, the chief of the fathers of the children of Israel, unto Jerusalem, to bring up the ark of the covenant of the LORD out of the City of David, which is Zion. Wherefore all the men of Israel assembled themselves unto the king in the feast which was in the seventh month" (II Chron. 5:2-3).

The time of this great gathering, the dedication of the temple, was the time of the Feast of Tabernacles, which convened in October (Lev. 23:34).

This could probably be said to be the greatest assembly that Israel had ever had. It was the dedication of the temple.

The ark of the covenant had probably been placed at the beginning on the threshingfloor of Araunah the Jebusite, which was before construction began on the temple. No doubt, when construction began, the ark had to be moved to another place in Jerusalem. Now it would be brought to the temple and ensconced in the Holy of Holies.

THE ARK OF THE COVENANT

Out of all the sacred vessels, and we speak of those that had been made for the tabernacle, the only one of these vessels now used in the temple seems to have been the ark of God.

It was placed, no doubt, in the center of the Holy of Holies, with the cherubim at either end looking down on the mercy seat; however, filling the room were the huge cherubim made of olivewood and overlaid with gold. Their wings touched in the middle with the back wings touching the back wall on either side. In other words, the wings of both cherubim touched each outer wall. Also, as stated, whereas the cherubim on the ark of the covenant looked down on the mercy seat, the faces of the giant cherubim looked outward, which signified redemption accomplished. Such portrayed these cherubim looking out on a world that is now absent of Satan and his minions of darkness, with the whole world, in one way or the other, serving God, whether by free will or of necessity. They look out on a world that is at peace, which is the first time such has ever happened. It will be during the coming kingdom age.

THE SACRIFICES

And all the elders of Israel came; and the Levites took up the ark. And they brought up the ark, and the tabernacle of the congregation, and all the holy vessels that were in the tabernacle, these did the priests and the Levites bring up. Also King Solomon, and all the congregation of Israel who were assembled unto him before the ark, sacrificed sheep and oxen, which could not be told nor numbered for multitude. And the priests brought in the ark of the covenant of the LORD unto His place, to the oracle of the house, into the most Holy Place, even under the wings of the cherubims: For the cherubims spread forth their wings over the place of the ark, and the cherubims covered the ark and the staves thereof above. And they drew out the staves of the ark, that the ends of the staves were seen from the ark before the oracle; but they were not seen without. And there it is unto this day. There was nothing in the ark save the two tables which Moses put therein at Horeb, when the LORD *made a covenant with the children of Israel, when they came out of Egypt* (II Chron. 5:4-10).

A TYPE OF THE CROSS

As it regards verse 4, these were priests who also were Levites, who were the only ones who could carry the ark. They were types of Christ, who alone is the door to the throne of God, of which the ark also was a type.

All of the *"holy vessels"* of verse 5 were by now a little over 600 years old. They, no doubt, were put *"among the treasures of the house of God"* in a separate chamber.

All the gold and precious stones in this magnificent temple could not redeem one precious soul; only the blood of Jesus could do such. Consequently, the thousands of animals slaughtered, which soaked the ground with blood, were an eternal type of the great price that would be paid at Calvary's Cross.

The staves being drawn out of the ark of verse 9 signified that it was to be moved no more. While Israel was in the wilderness, they were constantly moving. Now, that was over.

The phrase of verse 9, *"And there it is unto this day,"* proves that this section of II Chronicles was written before the destruction of the temple by Nebuchadnezzar.

When Paul, in Hebrews 9:4, mentioned the golden pot of manna and Aaron's rod being in the ark, he was speaking of the ark while in the tabernacle instead of the temple. It is not known when these two things were removed.

THE SACRIFICE OF SHEEP AND OXEN WITHOUT NUMBER

The sacrifice of this tremendous number of animals proclaimed the fact that as important as the temple was, still, the strength of Israel always had been, was, and ever would be the shed blood of the Lamb. Likewise, it is the strength of the church presently, at least for those who will believe.

Of course, the Holy Spirit knew exactly how many animals were offered in sacrifice; however, so many were offered that the number was not known as far as Solomon and others were concerned. There was a reason for this.

This great number offered signified the price that would be paid at Calvary and that it would be a finished work. In other words, the sacrifice of Christ would be complete, meaning that there would never be the need for another sacrifice.

It is impossible for one to honestly study the Bible and not come to the conclusion of the veracity of the Cross of Christ. It is the central theme of the entirety of the Word of God. With that being the case, it most definitely must be the central theme of the church.

Everything we receive from God comes through Jesus Christ by the means of the Cross. The Cross has made everything possible. If we do not understand this, then we do not really understand the Word of God.

All victory is found in the Cross! All prosperity is found in the Cross! All operation of the Holy Spirit is found in the Cross!

PRAISING AND THANKING THE LORD

And it came to pass, when the priests were come out of the Holy Place: (for all the priests who were present were sanctified, and did not then wait by course: Also the Levites which were the singers, all of them of Asaph, of Heman, of Jeduthun, with their sons and their brethren, being arrayed in white linen, having cymbals and psalteries and harps, stood at the east end of the altar, and with them an hundred and twenty priests sounding with trumpets:) It came even to pass, as the trumpeters and singers were as one, to make one sound to be heard in praising and thanking the LORD; *and when they lifted up their voice with the trumpets and cymbals and instruments of music, and praised the* LORD, *saying, For He is good; for His mercy endures forever: that then the house was filled with a cloud, even the house of the* LORD; *So that the priests could not stand to minister by reason of the cloud: for the glory of the* LORD *had filled the house* of God (II Chron. 5:11-14).

THE CLOUD

When the priests had placed the ark in the most Holy Place, they left, never to enter this place again, except for the visit of the high priest once a year, which was on the great Day of Atonement.

The *"altar"* pertained to the brazen altar, which sat in front of the temple. It was 30 feet wide and 30 feet long.

The phrase, *"Could not stand to minister by reason of the cloud,"* referred to the glory of God and meant that their knees buckled under them, and they fell to the floor because of the magnitude of the power of God being manifested.

"The glory of the LORD had filled the house," but now, Paul says that we are the temple of God (I Cor. 3:16) and that the Spirit of God dwells in us. The next question is, "Is He allowed to have His perfect way within our lives?" If He is, then the glory of the Lord will fill this house of God as well.

WORSHIP

When the ark was finally placed in the Holy of Holies, then the scores of singers and musicians began to worship and praise the Lord.

All music and singing began, in essence, with David as the Holy Spirit gave him the fundamentals of this most excellent way of worship. In fact, as it regards music and singing—at least that which is anointed by the Holy Spirit—such constitutes the highest form of worship and praise. We know this from the fact that the book of Psalms, which constitutes 150 songs—all written by the Holy Spirit and then given to various writers—presents the longest book in the Bible. In other words, for the Lord to devote this much time and space to this form of worship tells us of its vast significance. In fact, that's the reason that Satan comes against music and singing in the church as he does. If he can pervert that form of worship, he has greatly succeeded in wrecking the Gospel. Actually, the spiritual temperature of a church can be gauged by its worship, as it regards music and singing, or the lack thereof, or worse yet, the perversion thereof!

THE TEN COMMANDMENTS

The Scripture bears out that there were two tables in the ark of the covenant, which refers to the two stone tablets that contained the Ten Commandments, or as they are sometimes referred, *"the Ten Words."*

At other times, the ark of the covenant also contained a pot of manna and Aaron's rod that budded (Heb. 9:4).

What happened to these two?

We have no way of knowing what happened to the pot of manna and Aaron's rod; however, there was a reason that the two tablets containing the Ten Commandments were in the ark at that time.

The temple represented the kingdom age, which is to come, when Jesus will be ruling and reigning personally from Jerusalem over the entirety of the world. Inasmuch as He will be personally present, there will be no need for the pot of manna, which represented Christ as the Bread of Life, or Aaron's rod that budded, because that represented the resurrection of Christ, which was future when the rod was placed in the ark. Of course, it is obvious that the resurrection has long since taken place, making unnecessary that particular item.

As well, when Jesus comes back, the resurrection of all the saints will have already taken place.

THE MORAL PART OF THE LAW OF MOSES

However, the two tables containing the Ten Commandments represent moral laws which never change. They will be just as much incumbent upon the world during the time of the kingdom age as they were when they were first given. The Ten Commandments, which constitute the moral part of the law of Moses, actually present the central core of that law. Even though the entirety of the law was fulfilled in Christ, still, it is the Ten Commandments which constitute the righteousness of God and, as well, His standard by which all men will be judged.

The unredeemed do not know of such and, in fact, if it is brought to their attention, they express little concern. Still, all will answer to the law of God, whether it is answered in Jesus Christ by one giving one's heart to the Lord or at the great white throne judgment (Rev. 20:11-15). Its demands are inescapable!

THE GLORY OF THE LORD

The glory of the Lord filling the house constitutes the power of God.

Most people, sadly, do not understand the power of God. Most churches have no idea what the power of God actually is.

One must understand that the power of the Lord was so present that as the priests went about their duties, their knees buckled under them, and they fell to the floor. This is what our churches desperately need. This will bring conviction of sin as nothing else will. This is what the preacher needs. This is what every Christian needs.

We should call to our attention once again the fact that all of this great celebration, the dedication of the temple, and the glory thereof all began with the offering of the sacrifices, which were without number. This means that all of the proceedings were based on the shed blood of the lamb. This and this alone is the strength of the church, and we speak of the Cross.

The power of God, or presence of God, cannot be manifested unless the Cross of Christ is the object of faith. There may be that which disguises itself as the power of God, but unless it's based on the Cross, i.e., the shed blood of the Lamb, it is not really the power of God.

I will sing of my Redeemer,
And His wondrous love to me;
On the cruel Cross He suffered,
From the curse to set me free.

I will tell the wondrous story,
How my lost estate to save,
In His boundless love and mercy,
He the ransom freely gave.

I will praise my dear Redeemer,
His triumphant power I'll tell,
How the victory He gives,
Over sin, and death, and hell.

I will sing of my Redeemer,
And His heavenly love to me,
He from death to life has brought me,
Son of God, with Him to be.

Sing, O sing of my Redeemer,
With His blood He purchased me,
On the Cross He sealed my pardon,
Paid the debt, and made me free.

CHAPTER 11

JERUSALEM
AND DAVID

JERUSALEM AND DAVID

"THEN SAID SOLOMON, The L<small>ORD</small> *has said that He would dwell in the thick darkness. But I have built an house of habitation for You, and a place for Your dwelling forever. And the king turned his face, and blessed the whole congregation of Israel: and all the congregation of Israel stood"* (II Chron. 6:1-3).

SOLOMON'S MESSAGE

And he said, Blessed be the L<small>ORD</small> *God of Israel, who has with His hands fulfilled that which He spoke with His mouth to my father David, saying, Since the day that I brought forth My people out of the land of Egypt I chose no city among all the tribes of Israel to build an house in, that My name might be there; neither chose I any man to be a ruler over My people Israel: But I have chosen Jerusalem, that My name might be there; and have chosen David to be over my people Israel.*

Now it was in the heart of David my father to build an house for the name of the LORD God of Israel. But the LORD said to David my father, Forasmuch as it was in your heart to build an house for My name, you did well in that it was in your heart:

THE WORD OF THE LORD

Notwithstanding you shall not build the house; but your son which shall come forth out of your loins, he shall build the house for My name. The LORD therefore has performed His Word that He has spoken: for I am risen up in the room of David my father, and am set on the throne of Israel, as the LORD promised, and have built the house for the name of the LORD God of Israel. And in it have I put the ark, wherein is the covenant of the Lord, that He made with the children of Israel (II Chron. 6:4-11).

As it regards the Lord dwelling in thick darkness, Solomon may have taken this idea from the fact of God's appearance in darkness at Mount Sinai (Ex. 20:21).

For approximately 500 years, God had not chosen any particular place in Israel where a house should be built for Him, and neither had He chosen any man to be a permanent ruler over Israel. Now, He made it clear that He had chosen Jerusalem as the place of His headquarters on earth, and David was the one through whom all the future kings of Israel should come (II Sam., Chpt. 7; I Chron., Chpt. 17). This makes it clear that God did not choose Saul as He chose David. In fact, the Lord was pleased with David's motives as it regarded wanting to build a temple for the Lord.

JERUSALEM AND DAVID

The entirety of II Chronicles, Chapter 6, is broken into two parts:

1. The sermon of Solomon (Vss. 1-11).

2. The prayer of Solomon (Vss. 14-42).

In all of this, we see the manner and the way in which the Lord works. First of all, the Lord chose David to be over His people, Israel. The people didn't choose David; the Lord did. In fact, before David finally gained the throne, there was much difficulty. Satan always opposes, and does so greatly, that which is of God. Nevertheless, if the individual who is called will maintain his faith in Christ and what Christ has done at the Cross, the will of God will ultimately be brought about. It may be, and no doubt will be, even as John Newton wrote:

> *Through many dangers, toils, and snares,*
> *I have already come,*
> *But grace has brought me safe thus far,*
> *And grace shall lead me home.*

The Lord then chose Jerusalem as the city where He would place His name.

PLANS FOR THE TEMPLE

The Lord then gave to David the plans for the temple that was to be built—plans that included every detail. In other words, neither David nor Solomon added anything to what the Lord gave. He gave David the plans regarding how the building was to be constructed, and then the manner in which it was to be constructed. Nothing was left to chance or to the imagination of man.

The Lord then chose the exact spot where He wanted the temple erected. It was on the threshingfloor of Araunah the Jebusite, a part of the range of Mount Moriah. So, we see in all of this that everything was of God, and nothing was of man.

This is the manner and the way that God must work. In fact, He cannot use anything that originates with man, even the godliest of men, and for all the obvious reasons. It must be all of God, or it cannot be at all accepted by God.

THE MUSLIM WORLD

As is obvious and well-known, the Muslim world claims Jerusalem and, in fact, all of Israel, and, above all, they claim the temple mount that the Dome of the Rock presently occupies. Of course, this is Satan making his effort to thwart the plan of God.

However, let it ever be understood that whatever the Lord says—especially when the statement is unconditional, even as His choice of Jerusalem most definitely is—it's ultimately going to come out exactly as the Lord has stated. The Muslims need to understand that. It doesn't matter what the nations of the world try to do, what the Muslims try to do in their demonic endeavors, or what the United States does for that matter. The land referred to as "Israel" belongs to the Jews. As well, the temple site belongs to the Jews. Ultimately, despite all the efforts of the Muslims, Israel will occupy it all.

Those who set themselves against the Lord will not come out well, to say the least.

THE PRAYER OF SOLOMON

> *And he stood before the altar of the LORD in the presence of all the congregation of Israel, and spread forth his hands: For Solomon had made a brazen scaffold, of five cubits long, and five cubits broad, and three cubits high, and had set it in the midst of the court: and upon it he stood, and kneeled down upon his knees before all the congregation of Israel, and spread forth his hands toward heaven, And said, O LORD God of Israel, there is no God like You in the heaven, nor in the earth; which keeps covenant, and shows mercy unto Your servants, who walk before You with all their hearts: You who have kept with Your servant David my father that which You have promised him; and spoke with Your mouth, and have fulfilled it with Your hand, as it is this day. Now therefore, O LORD God of Israel, keep with Your servant David my father that which You have promised him, saying, There shall not fail you a man in My sight to sit upon the throne of Israel; yet so that your children take heed to their way to walk in My law, as you have walked before Me.*

Now then, O LORD God of Israel, let Your Word be verified, which you have spoken unto Your servant David. But will God in very deed dwell with men on the earth? behold, heaven and the heaven of heavens cannot contain You; how much less this house which I have built! Have respect therefore to the prayer of Your servant, and to his supplication, O LORD my God, to hearken unto the cry and the prayer which Your servant prays before You: That your eyes may be open upon this house day and night, upon the place whereof You have said that You would put Your name there; to hearken unto the prayer which Your servant prays toward this place.

PLEASE HEARKEN

Hearken therefore unto the supplications of Your servant, and of Your people Israel, which they shall make toward this place: hear You from Your dwelling place, even from heaven; and when You hear, forgive. If a man sin against his neighbor, and an oath be laid upon him to make him swear, and the oath come before Your altar in this house; Then hear You from heaven, and do, and judge Your servants, by requiting the wicked, by recompensing his way upon his own head; and by justifying the righteous, by giving him according to his righteousness. And if your people Israel be put to the worse before the enemy, because they have sinned against You; and shall return and confess Your name, and pray and make supplication before You in this house; Then hear You from the heavens and forgive the sin of Your people Israel, and bring them again unto the land which You gave to them and to their fathers. When the heaven is shut up, and there is no rain, because they have sinned against You; yet if they pray toward this place, and confess Your name, and turn from their sin, when You do afflict them; Then hear You from heaven, and forgive the sin of Your servants, and of Your people Israel, when You have taught them the good way, wherein they should walk; and send rain upon Your land, which You have given unto Your people for an inheritance.

JUDGMENT

If there be dearth in the land, if there be pestilence, if there be blasting, or mildew, locusts, or caterpillars; if their enemies besiege them in the cities of their land; whatsoever sore or whatsoever sickness there be: Then what prayer or what supplication soever shall be made of any man, or of all Your people Israel, when everyone shall know his own sore and his own grief, and shall spread forth his hands in this house: Then hear You from heaven Your dwelling place, and forgive, and render unto every man according unto all his ways, whose heart You know; (for You only know the hearts of the children of men:) That they may fear You, to walk in Your ways, so long as they live in the land which You gave unto our fathers. Moreover concerning the stranger, which is not of Your people Israel, but is come from a far country for Your great name's sake, and Your mighty hand, and Your stretched out arm; if they come and pray in this house; Then hear You from the heavens, even from Your dwelling place, and do according to all that the stranger calls to You for; that all people of the earth may know Your name, and fear You, as does Your people Israel, and may know that this house which I have built is called by Your name.

HAVE MERCY

If Your people go out to war against their enemies by the way that You shall send them, and they pray unto You toward this city which You have chosen, and the house which I have built for Your name; Then hear You from the heavens their prayer and their supplication, and maintain their cause. If they sin against You, (for there is no man which sins not,) and You be angry with them, and deliver them over before their enemies, and they carry them away captives unto a land far off or near; Yet if they bethink themselves in the land where they are carried captive, and turn and pray unto You in the land of their captivity, saying, We have sinned, we have done amiss, and have dealt wickedly; If they return to You with all their heart and with all their soul in the land of their captivity, whither they have carried them captives, and pray toward their land, which You gave unto their fathers, and toward the city which You have chosen, and toward the house which I have built for Your name: Then hear You from the heavens, even from Your dwelling place, their prayer and their supplications, and maintain their cause, and forgive Your people who have sinned against You. Now, my God, let, I beseech You, Your eyes be open, and let Your ears be attent unto the prayer that is made in this place. Now therefore arise, O LORD God, into Your resting place, You, and the ark of Your strength: let Your priests, O LORD God, be clothed with salvation, and let Your saints rejoice in goodness. O LORD God, turn not away the face of Your anointed: remember the mercies of David Your servant (II Chron. 6:12-42).

WHO KEEPS COVENANT

As it regards the Lord, verse 14 says, *"Which keeps covenant."* No man in all of eternity will ever be able to say that God has not kept His part of every agreement with men, or that He has not fulfilled every promise to them. Regrettably, Solomon himself, even after praying this prayer, did not take heed to walk in God's law.

As it regards God dwelling on this earth—as the question is asked in verse 18—the Lord most definitely will indeed dwell with men on this earth, and do so forever. Revelation, Chapters 21 and 22, proclaim this fact.

Prayer includes every thought and word from the heart that is godward. In this prayer, Solomon seems to have sensed the future of Israel prophetically. Sin is the only reason that Israel was ever defeated in battle. In fact, sin is to blame for all the troubles among men. As well, the Lord gave the land of Canaan to Israel and not the Arabs, even as this verse proclaims. Praying toward the temple, Jerusalem, and this land is referred to eight times in this prayer. It was done so because at that particular time, that was where God dwelt. Today, in this great dispensation of grace, it doesn't really matter which direction a person faces while praying. The reason is that the Lord, through the power of the Holy Spirit, now lives in the heart of born-again man (I Cor. 3:16), wherever such a man is, and not in some particular temple or building. This was all made possible by the Cross.

As well, the land between the river Euphrates and the Mediterranean Sea, and from the Red Sea on the south to Hamath on the north, is the only land promised in all of Scripture for all of the tribes of Israel. Theories that teach that America and England are new promised lands for Israel are all error. There is no hint of such in Scripture.

THE GENTILES

Solomon in his wisdom did not forget the Gentiles, whom God had in mind to bless from the very beginning of His calling Abraham, Isaac, and Jacob. All nations were to be blessed through Israel in her seed.

As well, this would imply the preaching of the Gospel, for how can individuals come to the God of Israel if they do not hear (Rom. 10:9-17; I Cor. 1:18-24)?

In fact, in the millennium and the new earth, all nations will go up to Jerusalem to pray and to worship exactly as they do now, if they so desire (Isa. 2:2-4; Zech. 8:23).

Solomon was right: all have sinned and come short of the glory of God (Rom. 3:23).

The word *saints* in the Hebrew means "men of grace," that is, those who are subjects of the grace of God.

This plainly shows that those in Old Testament times were under grace as well as we are in New Testament times. Actually, everyone who has been saved has been saved by grace, for there is no other way that an individual can be saved (Eph. 2:8).

And yet, grace as we know it under the new dispensation came by Jesus Christ, which means that it was all made possible by the Cross. Christ is always the source, while the Cross is always the means.

God's Anointed is the Messiah. Every blessing that we receive comes through the Lord Jesus Christ and, as stated, through what He has done for us at the Cross.

THE ALTAR

As Solomon began his prayer, he did so *"before the altar of the Lord."* This speaks of the great brazen altar on which sacrifices were offered constantly. It sat immediately in front of the temple.

Solomon praying his prayer at this particular place was not by accident but was designed by the Holy Spirit.

This should be a lesson to us as to the value of the Cross of Christ. Regrettably, the modern church tends to think it can live this life by devising its own means and ways. Failure is the guaranteed result.

Solomon knew that his prayer would be heard because of the sacrifices that had been offered upon the great altar. In fact, the Lord could be approached in no other way. As a result, he prayed this prayer of dedication very near the altar.

THE LORD GOD OF ISRAEL

In verse 14, Solomon extolled the *"LORD God of Israel."* He went on to state, *"There is no God like You in the heaven, nor in the earth; which keeps covenant, and shows mercy unto Your servants, who walk before You with all their hearts."*

The truth is, of all the nations on the earth at that time, Israel was the only one who knew the Lord of glory. To be sure, Jehovah alone is the Lord. There is no other.

Many nations referred to their "god" but, in reality, they had no god, only demon spirits. So, this made Israel, in a sense, the Lord of the earth. In fact, there was no other nation like these people.

As long as they served God, they could not be defeated by their enemies, and they knew nothing but freedom and prosperity. However, when they sinned and refused to repent, such was the ruin of these people, as sin is the ruin of any and all people.

DAVID

Some nine times in this chapter, Solomon referred to his father David. These nine times are:

1. He said the Lord spoke with His mouth to David (Vs. 4).

2. He chose David to be over His people Israel (Vs. 6).

3. He maintained, and rightly so, that it was in the heart of David to build the house of the Lord God (Vs. 7).

4. The Lord said to David, *"You shall not build the house; but your son which shall come forth out of your loins, he shall build the house for My name"* (Vs. 9).

5. Solomon proclaimed the fact that he was chosen by the Lord to occupy the throne when David died (Vs. 10).

6. He proclaimed the fact that the Lord kept every promise that He had given to David (Vs. 15).

7. The Lord promised David that his lineage would sit on the throne of Israel unless they failed to walk in God's law (Vs. 16).

8. Solomon implored the Lord that every promise made to David be kept (Vs. 17).

9. The Holy Spirit through Solomon used the term *"Your anointed."* Whether Solomon knew it or not, this spoke of the coming Messiah. It was attached to the request, *"Remember the mercies of David Your servant."* This referred to the fact that the Anointed One, the Messiah, would come from the lineage of David and, in fact, would be referred to as *"the Son of David"* (Vs. 42).

WILL GOD DWELL ON THE EARTH?

When Solomon asked the question of verse 18, *"But will God in very deed dwell with men on the earth?"* he had in mind the Lord dwelling between the mercy seat and the cherubim regarding this temple just finished. He knew that God would have to condescend to dwell in this building, considering *"the heaven of heavens cannot contain You; how much less this house which I have built!"*

In truth, God will dwell with men on the earth and will do so forever. Chapters 21 and 22 of Revelation bear this out. John said: *"And I heard a great voice out of heaven saying, Behold, the tabernacle of God is with men, and He will dwell with them, and they shall be His people, and God Himself shall be with them, and be their God"* (Rev. 21:3).

This will be in the coming perfect age, when the Lord will actually transfer His headquarters, so to speak, from heaven to earth.

Concerning that, John the Beloved said: *"And I John saw the Holy City, New Jerusalem, coming down from God out of heaven, prepared as a bride adorned for her husband"* (Rev. 21:2).

TOWARD JERUSALEM ...

In essence, all Jews were admonished to pray toward Jerusalem, irrespective of where they were in the world, which many do unto this day.

That was correct at that time, inasmuch as God dwelt in the temple in Jerusalem in the Holy of Holies.

Now, due to what Jesus did at the Cross, the Holy Spirit can dwell in the hearts and lives of believers wherever they might be; consequently, when prayer is offered now, no direction is specified, and for all the obvious reasons.

SIN

The Holy Spirit through Solomon proclaimed the fact that "sin" was the problem and that which caused so much difficulty and destruction. It is the same presently as it was then.

Every problem, in one way or the other, can be traced back to sin. While the person undergoing the difficulty may not have sinned at all, still, the cause of all trouble and heartache in this world and the cause of all problems and difficulties can be traced back to sin. As we say over and over, sin is the problem, and the solution is Jesus Christ and Him crucified. In fact, it is the only solution.

As well, Solomon implored the Lord to *"forgive the sin of Your people Israel,"* considering that they *"confess Your name, and pray and make supplication before You in this house"* (vss. 24-25). In other words, repentance will turn away the judgment of God.

It must be ever understood that God is unalterably opposed to sin, and to be sure, there is no one who gets by with sin.

THE CROSS

Any and every human being can allow Jesus Christ to serve as their mediator, which He will do by virtue of the Cross. This means that He took the penalty of sin, or else, such people are subject to the judgment of God. We can accept what Jesus did on our behalf at the Cross, or else, we will incur the wrath of God. The Scripture unequivocally says:

"For the wrath of God is revealed from heaven against all ungodliness and unrighteousness of men, who hold the truth in unrighteousness" (Rom. 1:18).

Unfortunately, sin is hardly mentioned in the modern church because to do so, it is said, might offend the congregation.

Telling a person who has cancer that everything is alright when, in reality, the individual is dying, is not doing that person a favor. Let's say it again: The problem is sin! The solution is Jesus Christ and what He did at the Cross. There is no other solution simply because there need not be any other solution.

GENTILES

Solomon referred to Gentiles as *"strangers."* No doubt, the Holy Spirit moved upon Solomon to pray this prayer and its content. The Lord was quick to include the stranger and the blessings that could come from seeking His face at this *house.* In other words, Gentiles were encouraged to come. In fact, there was an entire court set aside for the Gentiles to which they could come and pray to the Lord.

It was in this court, the court of the Gentiles, that Jesus ran out the moneychangers. In essence, the Jews had taken over this court and had set up all types of stalls to change money and to do other things. In other words, it was almost impossible for any Gentile to come to this place and pray due to the activity. Jesus ran them all out (Jn. 2:13-17).

Israel was raised up by the Lord for three major purposes. They were:

1. To give the world the Word of God. Every writer in the Bible is Jewish, with the possible exception of Luke. However, it is my conclusion that Luke was Jewish as well. Israel succeeded in this all-important task.

2. To serve as the womb of the Messiah, which refers to the first advent of the Lord Jesus Christ and Him being born of the Virgin Mary in Bethlehem. This was brought about, as well, but sadly and regrettably, Israel crucified her Messiah. They have suffered untold agony from that day until this because of that action.

3. Israel was also ordained by God to serve as a missionary to the Gentile world. In a sense, they succeeded in this through the Apostle Paul, as well as the original Twelve and others. Of course, most of Israel rejected the Lord, but one day soon, the entirety of the Jewish people, and we speak of those from all over the world, will accept Jesus Christ as Saviour and Lord. However, that will not be until the second coming. Then, the entire nation will serve as missionaries, going out all over the world to make the world aware that the Messiah, the Lord Jesus Christ, and their Saviour has come (Isa. 66:18-20).

THE ANOINTED

When the word *"anointed"* is used in the manner in which it has been used in verse 42, it is speaking of the coming Redeemer, the Lord Jesus Christ. Christ would come through the lineage of David exactly as He had promised the king of Israel (II Sam., Chpt. 7).

So, Solomon began his prayer at the altar, i.e., the Cross, and closed it with the coming Messiah, the Lord Jesus Christ. How fitting!

I stand all amazed at the love Jesus offers me,
Confused at the grace that so fully He proffers me;
I tremble to know that for me He was crucified—
That for me, a sinner, He suffered, He bled and died.

I marvel that He would descend from His throne divine,
To rescue a soul so rebellious and proud as mine;
That He should extend His great love unto such as I;
Sufficient to own, to redeem, and to justify.

I think of His hands pierced and bleeding to pay that debt!
Such mercy, such love and devotion can I forget?
No, no, I will praise and adore at the mercy–seat,
Until at the glorified throne I kneel at His feet.

CHAPTER 12

THE GLORY OF
THE LORD

CHAPTER TWELVE

THE GLORY OF THE LORD

"NOW WHEN SOLOMON HAD made an end of praying, the fire came down from heaven, and consumed the burnt offering and the sacrifices; and the glory of the LORD filled the house. And the priests could not enter into the house of the LORD, because the glory of the LORD had filled the LORD's house. And when all the children of Israel saw how the fire came down, and the glory of the LORD upon the house, they bowed themselves with their faces to the ground upon the pavement, and worshipped, and praised the LORD, saying, For He is good; for His mercy endures forever" (II Chron. 7:1-3).

THE FIRE FELL

Verse 1 is additional to I Kings 8:63-64, and shows the Lord's divine acceptance of the sacrifices until Christ should come to offer Himself as the one great, eternal sacrifice for all of humanity.

The fire of God from heaven has fallen several times on such occasions (Gen. 4:4; 15:17; Lev. 9:24; I Chron. 21:26; I Ki. 18:38).

As it regards all the sacrifices that were offered, we should learn from this that the *"glory of the LORD"* can only come through Calvary. On the Day of Pentecost, approximately 1,000 years later, the fire fell from heaven in a way that it had never fallen previously.

In Old Testament times, it fell upon the sacrifice. Now that the sacrifice, the Lord Jesus Christ, has been offered, the same fire can now culminate in the Holy Spirit coming into the heart and life of the believer, but not with judgment, for the judgment has been expended on Christ. However, this *Pentecostal fire* will definitely correct the believer (Mat. 3:11-12; Acts 2:3).

FIRE CAME DOWN FROM HEAVEN

George Williams said, "The fire that consumed the burnt offering of the dedication of the temple 'came down from heaven,' but the fire that consumed the burnt offering – offering at the dedication of the tabernacle 'came out from before the Lord,' that is, came out from between the cherubim within the most Holy Place. But in coming out from, and passing through the tabernacle, it did not burn it, for that tent was Christ.

"This is characteristic. The fire from the tabernacle is Christ in His first advent; the fire from heaven, Christ in His second advent."

The fire that came down from heaven also showed the divine acceptance of sacrifices until the Messiah should come to offer Himself as the one, great, eternal sacrifice for all men.

The scene of this chapter was one of grandeur and awe. It depicted the king, with uplifted hands, kneeling in royal robes upon the brazen platform and the vast multitude prostrate upon the ground. As well, it showed the fire from heaven consuming the sacrifice upon the brazen altar and the cloud of the glory of Jehovah filling the house of Jehovah. This all formed a scene of mysterious splendor such as the world had never witnessed.

THE DWELLING PLACE OF GOD

The fact that this was the only temple in the whole world in which the one true God was worshipped adds to the moral grandeur of the scene.

The spiritual knowledge that Solomon possessed and the visible fire that burned upon the altar came from heaven; both originated there, and both were divine. Man could not have created that miraculous fire or that equally miraculous knowledge. The fact of the existence of God was attested by the fire. No other nation possessed this knowledge of God, and neither could any nation by reason or culture obtain such knowledge. It could only be had by revelation. Thus, both the fire and the teaching of the prayer came from heaven.

THE BURNT OFFERING

The *"burnt offering"* on the altar signified that God gave His all in the person of Jesus Christ. The fire upon that sacrifice signified the judgment of God that should have come upon us, but instead, would fall upon the perfect offering for sin, the Christ of Calvary. Does one think that all of these sacrifices were merely for the act of ceremony or ritual? Hardly!

First of all, the voluminous number of sacrifices pictured and portrayed the coming Redeemer; therefore, they were of utmost significance. Secondly, all of this portrayed the fact that Israel's safety and protection, as well as her freedom and prosperity, rested solely upon the shed blood of the Lamb. When will the modern church see this?

In the modern church, the Cross is little more than a good luck charm and little more than a part of the whole, and a small part at that. Cannot we see from the Word of God that all blessing, all prosperity, and all the leading and guidance of the Holy Spirit, in fact, everything that we receive from God, comes to us through Jesus Christ and by the means of the Cross? If we can't see that, it's simply because we willfully do not desire to see it.

THE GLORY OF THE LORD
FILLED THE HOUSE

The *"glory of the LORD"* can only come through Calvary. In too many churches, Calvary has been relegated to second or even third place, or completely ignored altogether, which is mostly the case. Let it ever be understood that God's glory cannot rest upon anything except the precious shed blood of Jesus Christ. If we want the glory of the Lord to fill the house, which now speaks of our person, we must place the preeminence on Calvary. Paul said that he would glory in the Cross

(Gal. 6:14). He also said, *"I determined not to know anything among you save Jesus Christ, and Him crucified"* (I Cor. 2:2).

The *"house"* presently is our physical body, our hearts, and our lives. Paul also said concerning this:

> *Know you not that you are the temple of God* (where the Holy Spirit abides), *and that the Spirit of God dwells in you?* (That makes the born-again believer His permanent home.)

The apostle went on to say,

> *If any man defile the temple of God* (our physical bodies must be a living sacrifice, which means that we stay holy by ever making the Cross the object of our faith [Rom. 12:1]), *him shall God destroy* (to fail to function in God's prescribed order [the Cross] opens the believer up to Satan, which will ultimately result in destruction); *for the temple of God is holy, which temple you are.* (We are 'holy' by virtue of being 'in Christ.' We remain holy by the work of the Holy Spirit, who demands that our faith ever be in the Cross, which has made all of this possible) (I Cor. 3:16-17) (The Expositor's Study Bible).

THE HOLY SPIRIT

The fact that the Holy Spirit now abides permanently within the hearts and lives of all believers was made possible by the Cross of Christ. The Cross pictures and proclaims the shed blood of Christ, which atoned for all sin, past, present, and future, at least for those who believe. Before the Cross, animal blood served as a stopgap measure, so to speak; however, animal blood was and is woefully insufficient. It could never cleanse sin or serve as an atoning factor as it regarded the principle of substitution, because animal blood was itself only a substitute. With that being the case, the sin debt was not lifted, meaning that man was still under the dread plague, even the godliest among those of Old Testament times. Actually, whenever believers died in those times, their souls and spirits did not go to heaven, but rather down into paradise, referred to as Abraham's bosom, which was actually a place in a part of hell itself. True, Jesus said there was a great gulf between paradise and the burning side of hell, but still, before the Cross, all believers were, in a measure, held captive by Satan (Lk. 16:19-31).

That's the reason that Paul said concerning Jesus,

When He ascended up on high (the ascension), *He led captivity captive* (liberated the souls in paradise; before the Cross, despite being believers, they were still held captive by Satan because the blood of bulls and goats could not take away the sin debt owed by all; but when Jesus died on the Cross, the sin debt was paid, and now He made all of these His captives), *and gave gifts unto men.* (These 'gifts' include all the attributes of Christ, all made possible by the Cross.)

THE CROSS OF CHRIST

(Now that He ascended (mission completed), *what is it but that He also descended first into the lower parts of the earth?* (Immediately before His ascension to glory, which would

be done in total triumph, He first went down into paradise
to deliver all the believing souls in that region, which He
did) (Eph. 4:8-9) (The Expositor's Study Bible).

As it should be understood, everything hinged on the Cross
of Christ. This means that every single believer who was in paradise was dependent solely on the great work that Jesus would
carry out at the Cross. This would release them from this place
and give them access to heaven, which Christ afforded Himself.

The phrase, *"He led captivity captive,"* is strange, but what it
means is this:

CAPTIVITY CAPTIVE

No one knows how many people were in paradise, but quite
possibly, there were millions there. Because animal blood was
insufficient to rid them of the sin debt, as stated, they were actually
captives of Satan. While Satan could not harm them and could
not take them over into the burning side of hell, still, due to the
fact that the sin debt remained, this meant that they were in the
domain of Satan himself. Actually, there is no record that Satan
personally was ever in paradise or the burning side of hell, but
most definitely, many of his demon spirits and fallen angels were.

When Jesus died on the Cross, thereby, atoning for all sin,
past, present, and future, in effect, this liberated all the believers in totality. To make certain that they were liberated, Jesus
went into this place Himself and made each one of them His
captives and took them with Him to glory.

Now, when a believer dies, due to the Cross, in that the sin debt is paid, such a believer instantly goes to be with Christ in the portals of glory (Phil. 1:23).

THE LORD IS GOOD, HIS MERCY ENDURES FOREVER

The Lord is good! Every believer knows that, and the whole world should know that as well.

If one wants to know who and what God the Father is like, one only has to look at the Lord Jesus Christ in the four Gospels. Jesus said:

If you had known Me, you should have known My Father also (means, 'If you had learned to know Me spiritually and experientially, you should have known that I and the Father are one' i.e., one in essence and unity, and not in number)*: and from henceforth you know Him, and have seen Him* (when one truly sees Jesus, one truly sees the Father; as stated, they are 'one' in essence). *Philip said unto Him, Lord, show us the Father, and it suffices us* (like Philip, all, at least for the most part, want to see God, but the far greater majority reject the only manner and way to see Him, which is through Jesus).

JESUS CHRIST AND GOD THE FATHER

Jesus said unto him, Have I been so long with you, and yet have you not known Me, Philip? (Reynolds says, 'There is no right understanding of Jesus Christ until the Father is actually seen in Him.') *He who has seen Me has seen the Father* (presents the very embodiment of who and what the Messiah would be; if we want to know what God is like, we need only look at the Son); *and how do you say then, Show us the Father? Do you believe not that I am in the Father, and the Father in Me?* (The key is 'believing.') *the words that I speak unto you I speak not of Myself* (the words which came out of the mouth of the Master are, in fact, those of the heavenly Father): *but the Father who dwells in Me, He does the works* (the Father does such through the Holy Spirit). *Believe me that I am in the Father, and the Father in Me* (once again places faith as the vehicle and Jesus as the object): *or else believe Me for the very works' sake* (presents a level which should be obvious to all and includes present observation as well) (Jn. 14:7-11) (The Expositor's Study Bible).

WHAT IS MERCY?

In the Hebrew, the word *mercy* could probably be expressed best by the words *loving-kindness.*

It denotes devotion to a covenant, and so of God, His covenant-love (Ps. 89:28). However, God's faithfulness to a graciously established relationship with Israel or an individual, despite human unworthiness and affection, readily passes over into His mercy. In fact, this steady, persistent refusal of God to wash His hands of wayward Israel is the essential meaning of the Hebrew word *mercy*, which is translated "loving-kindness."

In the New Testament, "mercy" could probably be defined as "compassion to one in need or helpless distress, or in debt and without claim to favorable treatment." God is referred to as *"the Father of mercies"* (II Cor. 1:3; Ex. 34:6; Neh. 9:17; Ps. 86:15; 103:8-14; Joel 2:13; Jonah 4:2).

His compassion is over all that He has made (Ps. 145:9), and it is because of His mercy that we are saved (Eph. 2:4; Titus 3:5). Jesus was often *"moved with compassion,"* and He bids us to be *"merciful, as your Father also is merciful"* (Lk. 6:36; Mat. 18:21, 27).

The Scripture says that the merciful are blessed and will receive mercy (Mat. 5:7; James 2:13).

(The above material on mercy was derived from the New Bible Dictionary.)

RECIPIENTS OF MERCY

Mercy is afforded the undeserving, as no one deserves God's mercy, strictly by and through the Cross of Christ. In fact, everything comes to the believer by the means of the Cross, with our Lord as the source.

The Holy Spirit gave over the entirety of the 136TH Psalm to the mercy of God, *"For His mercy endures forever."* It is not known who wrote this psalm, but more than likely, the author was David. In fact, the people of Israel basically quoted verse 1 of the 136TH Psalm in their praises. So, this means it was written by the time they quoted it and, as stated, more than likely, by David. I quote from The Expositor's Study Bible:

Oh give thanks unto the LORD; for He is good: for His mercy endures forever. (We must never forget that 'God is good!' Therefore, He is merciful.) *Oh give thanks unto the God of gods: for His mercy endures forever.* (The Hebrew for 'God of gods' is 'Elohim of the Elohim.' He is speaking here of the Trinity of which all are equal. In the Trinity, 'His mercy endures forever.') *Oh give thanks to the Lord of lords: for His mercy endures forever.* (The Hebrew is 'Adonim of the Adonim,' which means 'Sovereign of the sovereigns; Master of the masters; Ruler of the rulers.')

GOD THE CREATOR

To Him who alone does great wonders: for His mercy endures forever. (God alone can perform constructive miracles.) *To Him who by wisdom made the heavens: for His mercy endures forever.* (This ascribes to God all the planetary systems.) *To Him who stretched out the earth above the waters: for His mercy endures forever* (who separated the land and the seas; the attention which the Holy Spirit gives to the mercy of God in all of these verses is beautifully amazing, and rightly so!). *To Him who made great lights: for His mercy endures forever* (God is 'light,' so the creation of light is a natural result of His divine person): *The sun to rule by day: for His mercy endures forever: The moon and stars to rule by night: for His mercy endures forever.* (The Holy Spirit is telling us here that all of creation, and its ordered existence, is a result of the mercy of God.) *To Him who smote Egypt in their firstborn: for His mercy endures forever* (this tells us that all judgments poured out on Egypt were a result of mercy; the Lord could have smitten Egypt at the beginning; however, He sent judgments, including the death of the firstborn, all in order to get them to repent, but to no avail): *And brought out Israel from among them: for His mercy endures forever* (to bring Israel out was not only an act of mercy for Israel, but for Egypt as well):

ALMIGHTY POWER

With a strong hand, and with a stretched out arm: for His mercy endures forever. (The 'strong hand' and the 'stretched out arm,' which God used to deliver Israel, were all because of mercy.) *To Him who divided the Red Sea into parts: for His mercy endures forever* (this passage destroys the myth that the Red Sea at the place of the crossing was only a few inches deep): *And made Israel to pass through the midst of it: for His mercy endures forever* (it took faith for Israel to pass through; they had to believe that God, who had made this path through the sea, would, as well, continue to defy the laws of gravity by holding the water up like two walls on either side): *But overthrew Pharaoh and his host in the Red Sea: for His mercy endures forever.* (The indication here is that Pharaoh drowned along with his army.)

GREAT MERCY

To Him who led His people through the wilderness: for His mercy endures forever. (God intended for the stay in the wilderness to be of short duration – a few months to two years at the most. The forty years was because of Israel's unbelief and rebellion.) *To Him who smote great kings: for His mercy endures forever* (this speaks of Pharaoh as well as the kings mentioned in the following verses): *And killed famous kings: for His mercy endures forever: Sihon king of the Amorites: for His mercy endures forever: And Og the king of Bashan: for His mercy endures forever* (tradition says that Sihon was the brother of King Og; both were Amorites; they were giants of the race of the Rephaim at the time of the conquest of Palestine): *And gave their land for an heritage: for His mercy endures forever: Even an heritage unto Israel His servant: for His mercy endures forever.* (Og's territory was given to the half-tribe of Manasseh [Deut. 3:13]. Sihon's territory was given to the tribes of Reuben and Gad [Num. 32:23-38; Josh. 13:10].)

THE LORD REMEMBERS

Who remembered us in our low estate: for His mercy endures forever (God remembers His mercy and grace and forgets our sins; man forgets God's mercy and grace and remembers our sins): *And has redeemed us from our enemies: for His mercy endures forever.* (The word 'redeemed' means to rescue and to break the power of the one who has us bound, namely Satan. This redemption is so powerful that it not only redeems us, but also destroys our enemies.) *Who gives food to all flesh: for His mercy endures forever.* (The 'food' addressed here pertains not only to spiritual food, but also to natural food.) *Oh give thanks unto the God of heaven: for His mercy endures forever.* (As 'His mercy endures forever,' likewise, our 'thanks unto Him' should endure forever.) (Ps. 136:1-26).

SACRIFICES

Then the king and all the people offered sacrifices before the LORD. And King Solomon offered a sacrifice of twenty and two thousand oxen, and an hundred and twenty thousand sheep: so the king and all the people dedicated the house of God. And the priests waited on their offices: the Levites also with instruments of music of the LORD, which David the king had made to praise the LORD, because His mercy endures forever, when David praised by their ministry; and the priests sounded trumpets before them, and all Israel stood. Moreover Solomon hallowed the middle of the court that was before the house of the LORD: for there he offered burnt offerings, and the fat of the peace offerings, because the brazen altar which Solomon had made was not able to receive the burnt offerings, and the meat offerings, and the fat. Also at the same time Solomon kept the feast seven days, and all Israel with him, a very great congregation, from the entering in of Hamath unto the river of Egypt. And in the eighth day they made a solemn assembly: for they kept the dedication of the altar seven days, and the feast seven days. And on the three and twentieth day of the seventh month he sent the people away into their tents, glad and merry in heart for the goodness that the LORD had shown unto David, and to Solomon, and to Israel His people. Thus Solomon finished the house of the LORD, and the king's house: and all that came into Solomon's heart to make in the house of the LORD, and in his own house, he prosperously effected (II Chron. 7:4-11).

THE SHED BLOOD OF THE LAMB

The tremendous number of sacrifices offered portrayed the fact to Israel that her great blessing was built on the foundation of the shed blood of the lamb. Even though the number of sacrifices offered was staggering, still, it could not begin to portray Calvary. The blood of bulls and goats could never take away sins (Heb. 10:4); nevertheless, these sacrifices did point to the Lamb of God, who would take away all sin (Jn. 1:29).

The worship, heavily anchored in the sacrifices, portrays the fact that Spirit-led music and singing accompany the Cross and, in fact, are made possible by the Cross.

The burnt offerings typified the perfection of Christ being given to the sinner. The *"fat"* typified the very best that God has in the offering up of His Son. The peace offerings typified that peace had been restored as a result of the burnt offering.

The middle court, which was the court of women, had to also be used for sacrifices because the area around the brazen altar was too small, considering the great number of sacrifices being offered.

There was a Feast of Dedication of the temple, which was seven days long, and then Solomon also kept the Feast of

Tabernacles for an additional seven days, making altogether 14 days of feasting at that time.

Joy always follows proper worship, which is always anchored in the Cross, typified by the sacrifices.

THE SACRIFICES

Speaking of the number of sacrifices, verse 5 says, *"Twenty and two thousand oxen, and an hundred and twenty thousand sheep."* The brook Kidron that ran between the Mount of Olives and the temple site ran red with blood, showing Israel that her great blessing was built on the foundation of the shed blood of Christ.

Even though the number of sacrifices offered was staggering, still, it could not even begin to portray Calvary. While the blood of bulls and goats could not take away sins, still, they served as a type, a symbol, of the One, the Lamb of God, who would and, in fact, did take away all sin. He did so by the offering of Himself as a sacrifice on the Cross of Calvary (Jn. 1:29).

It has been asked why Solomon offered this many sacrifices. The law of Moses did not require such. Even the Scripture doesn't say. I believe that Solomon was led by the Lord in this which He did. He was so very much aware of the true strength of Israel, which was, as stated, the shed blood of the Lamb, all typified by the sacrificial offerings of these clean animals, that the staggering number offered typified several things:

A TYPE OF CALVARY

- No number offered, no matter how high it would have been, could have even remotely compared with the one offering of Calvary.

- Even the staggering number offered could not take away sins, not even one sin (Heb. 10:4). Still, the number involved did serve as a symbol that the blood shed by the one sacrifice of Calvary would suffice for all of mankind and for all time, at least for all who would believe (Jn. 3:16).

- The tremendous number of sacrifices offered, as well, speaks of the preciousness of the blood that would be shed at Calvary's Cross. It is precious in that it serves as the price paid for every single soul who will believe, which places its worth beyond the comprehension of man.

- Incidentally, regarding the number of sacrifices offered, the value in today's currency would have been close to $60 million.

BURNT OFFERINGS, PEACE OFFERINGS, AND MEAT OFFERINGS

The whole burnt offerings were probably the most common type of offerings presented. As we have previously stated, this particular offering represented Christ giving His all, even as the sin offering represented the sinner giving Christ the totality of his sin.

Whenever whole burnt offerings or sin or trespass offerings were presented, they were almost always followed by peace offerings.

The peace offering was the one offering of which very little was burnt on the altar (the fat), with the bulk being eaten by the priests, and especially by the one who presented the offering. The idea was that since the matter of sin had been settled between God and the individual as a result of the sin offering, which typified Christ, now there could be rejoicing in the eating of the peace offering, inasmuch as peace was now restored because the sin had been covered.

The scene at the dedication of the temple must have been beautiful to behold. Tens of thousands of people partaking of the peace offerings—in other words, holding a feast for their family and friends as the Scripture provided for them to do—presented a perfect type of what Christ would do in the hearts and lives of those who would trust Him.

THE EATING OF THE PEACE OFFERING

The priests were commanded to eat portions of the offerings. Now, as it regarded the peace offering, the people themselves were also able to participate. This was the only offering in which they could participate in this manner. All of this has a great scriptural meaning in Christ.

In essence, this is what Jesus was talking about when He said to Israel:

> *Except you eat the flesh of the Son of Man, and drink His blood, you have no life in you* (this terminology addresses the Cross; Christ would give Himself on the Cross for the salvation of mankind; to fully believe in Him and what He did for us is what He means here; however, this verse tells us the degree of believing that is required; it refers to the Cross being the total object of one's belief; failing that, there is no life in you). *Whoso eats My flesh, and drinks My blood, has eternal life* (once again Christ reiterates the fact that if the Cross is the total object of one's faith, such a person has 'eternal life'); *and I will raise him up at the last day* (constitutes the fourth time this is spoken by Christ; consequently, the believer has a fourfold assurance of the resurrection).

THE CROSS OF CHRIST

> *For My flesh is meat indeed, and My blood is drink indeed* (the idea is that one must continue eating and drinking, even on a daily basis, which, of course, is symbolic, which speaks of bearing the Cross daily [Lk. 9:23]). *He who eats My flesh, and drinks My blood, dwells in Me, and I in him* (the only way that one can dwell in Christ and Christ in him, which guarantees a victorious, overcoming life, is for the Cross to ever be the object of faith and, as stated, on a daily basis) (Jn. 6:53-56) (The Expositor's Study Bible).

The idea is that when one fully believes in Christ and what He did at the Cross, in the mind of God, one literally is placed in Christ. This means that whatever Christ is, we are as well. The union is to be total, close, and complete, hence, Jesus praying, *"That they may be one, as We are"* (Jn. 17:11).

The eating of the flesh of the Son of God and the drinking of His blood was not meant, as should be obvious, to be taken literally. The terminology is used in this fashion to emphasize the validity of the Cross. It speaks of the crucifixion of Christ and one's faith in that finished work (Rom. 6:3-5). It was typified, as stated, in the eating of the peace offerings.

MEAT OFFERINGS

The meat offerings probably would have been better translated "thank offerings." In fact, they were the only offerings of the fivefold offerings that contained no flesh. It was bread that was made in a certain way. No leaven or honey was permitted (Lev. 2:11), only cakes being offered.

The offerer was responsible for bringing the prepared loaves or wafers to the sanctuary. The priests burned one handful on the altar, and the rest was his to eat (Lev. 2:2).

The meat offering or cereal offering normally accompanied every burnt offering. The quantities of fine flour and oil were fixed according to the animal being sacrificed. It is believed that peace offerings were always accompanied by cereal offerings. The priests ate a part of these offerings, with the rest being eaten by the offerer with the flesh of the sacrificial animal. All of this was a type of Christ, which was totally fulfilled when He came to this world and gave Himself on the Cross as a complete and total sacrifice for the sins of man.

As much as it being a type of Christ, it must be emphasized, it was a type of Christ as it regarded what He would do for us at the Cross.

GLAD AND MERRY IN HEART

When the Cross of Christ, i.e., the sacrifice of Christ, is the foundation of all that we are and all that we do, to be sure, it will produce that which is *"glad and merry in heart."* This is something that money cannot buy, secular education cannot give, and that is beyond the pale of human endeavor, that is, as we look at personal ability. And yet, it is an automatic place and position when the Cross of Christ becomes the foundation of all that we are.

Presently, the spirit of depression among Christians is at an all time high. This is not the way that it is supposed to be. Sometime back, while preaching on a Sunday morning at Family Worship Center, I was dealing with oppression, which is the first cousin, if not the twin brother, of depression. While Satan cannot possess a believer, he most definitely can oppress a believer. The difference is, possession is within, while oppression is without.

OPPRESSION

I think I can say without fear of contradiction or exaggeration that every single believer at one time or another has experienced satanic oppression. The Scripture says concerning oppression: *"How God anointed Jesus of Nazareth with the Holy Spirit and with power: who went about doing good, and healing all who were oppressed of the Devil; for God was with Him"* (Acts 10:38).

Oppression causes emotional disturbance, which, within itself, can cause a raft of problems with the individual. It causes nervous disorders and, as well, certain types of sicknesses. As would be obvious, it destroys the peace, the security, and the assurance of the individual.

As I was preaching that Sunday morning at Family Worship Center and, as stated, dealing with this very subject, all of a sudden, something dawned on me that had not previously come to my attention.

The Lord gave me the revelation of the Cross in 1997, or I might say, began to give this great revelation to me at that time. Whereas I was troubled with demonic oppression quite often before that time, I suddenly realized, even while I was preaching, that I had not experienced one single solitary moment of oppression since my faith had been anchored securely in the Cross of Christ. In other words, the Lord Jesus Christ and what He did for us at the Cross had become my object of faith in totality. There was no more oppression.

Why?

OPPRESSION AND THE CROSS OF CHRIST

It was at the Cross that every demon spirit was defeated, along with Satan himself. The Scripture says concerning this:

Buried with Him in baptism (does not refer to water baptism, but rather to the believer baptized into the death of Christ, which refers to the crucifixion and Christ as our substitute [Rom. 6:3-4]), *wherein also you are risen with Him through the faith of the operation of God, who has raised Him from the dead.* (This does not refer to our future physical resurrection, but to that spiritual resurrection from a sinful state into divine life. We died with Him, we are buried with Him, and we rose with Him [Rom. 6:3-5], and herein lies the secret to all spiritual victory.) *And you, being dead in your sins and the uncircumcision of your flesh* (speaks of spiritual death, [i.e., 'separation from God'], which sin does!), *has He quickened together with Him* (refers to being made spiritually alive, which is done through being 'born again'), *having forgiven you all trespasses* (the Cross made it possible for all manner of sins to be forgiven and taken away);

SATISFIED THE LAW THAT WAS AGAINST US

Blotting out the handwriting of ordinances that was against us (pertains to the law of Moses, which was God's standard of righteousness that man could not reach), *which was contrary to us* (law is against us simply because we are unable to keep its precepts, no matter how hard we try), *and took it out of the way* (refers to the penalty of the law being removed), *nailing it to His Cross* (the law with its decrees was abolished in Christ's death as if crucified with Him); *And having spoiled principalities and powers* (Satan and all of his henchmen were defeated at the Cross by Christ atoning for all sin; sin was the legal right Satan had to hold man in captivity; with all sin atoned, he has no more legal right to hold anyone in bondage) *He* (Christ) *made a show of them openly* (what Jesus did at the Cross was in the face of the whole universe), *triumphing over them in it.* (The triumph is complete, and it was all done for us, meaning we can walk in power and perpetual victory due to the Cross) (Col. 2:12-15) (The Expositor's Study Bible).

THE CROSS

It was at the Cross where Satan and all of his minions of darkness were defeated; consequently, the Holy Spirit works entirely within the framework of the finished work of Christ. In other words, He works entirely within those boundaries and will not work outside of those boundaries. It is the Cross that provides the legal means for the Holy Spirit to abide within our hearts and lives, and to do with us and for us what He alone can do. In fact, this is such an ironclad truth that the Holy Spirit refers to it as a law. Listen to Paul:

For the law (that which we are about to give is a law of God, devised by the Godhead in eternity past [I Pet. 1:18-20]; this law, in fact, is 'God's prescribed order of victory') *of the Spirit* (Holy Spirit, i.e., 'the way the Spirit works') *of life* (all life comes from Christ but through the Holy Spirit [Jn. 16:13-14]) *in Christ Jesus* (any time Paul uses this term or one of its derivatives, he is, without fail, referring to what Christ did at the Cross, which makes this 'life' possible) *has made me free* (given me total victory) *from the law of sin and death* (these are the two most powerful laws in the universe; the 'law of the Spirit of life in Christ Jesus alone is stronger than the 'law of sin and death'; this means that if the believer attempts to live for God by any manner other than faith in Christ and the Cross, he is doomed to failure) (Rom. 8:2) (The Expositor's Study Bible).

RESURRECTION LIFE

The secret to living for God in this more abundant life, and enjoying all of that for which Christ paid such a price at Calvary's Cross, is resurrection life.

What is resurrection life?

Listen again to Paul:

For if we have been planted together (with Christ) *in the likeness of His death* (Paul proclaims the Cross as the instrument through which all blessings come; consequently, the Cross must ever be the object of our faith, which gives the Holy Spirit latitude to work within our lives), *we shall be also in the likeness of His resurrection* (we can have the 'likeness of His resurrection,' i.e., 'live this resurrection life,' only as long as we understand the 'likeness of His death,' which refers to the Cross as the means by which all of this is done (Rom. 6:5) (The Expositor's Study Bible).

Coming up as a young preacher in a particular full Gospel denomination, from time to time, Frances and I would hear preachers talking about "living the resurrection life."

LIVING THE RESURRECTION LIFE

I found out later that none of these preachers really knew or understood what that term actually meant—*living the resurrection life.* If you had asked them, they would have referred to works of the law of some kind that the believer is supposed to carry out, which would enable such a believer to live the resurrection life. Actually, their statements in some way, at least those that I heard, always repudiated the Cross. In other words, they would say they had no interest in the Cross, only the resurrection.

In verse 5 of Romans, Chapter 6, the Holy Spirit through Paul emphatically states, *"For if we have been planted together in the likeness of His death,"* which refers to the fact that all victory is in the Cross. That's where we go wrong; we try to place the center and circumference of victory in other things. It really doesn't matter what the other things are, or how valuable they are in their own right. The believer must understand that all victory, and we mean all victory, is found exclusively in the Cross of Christ. In other words, before we can enjoy resurrection life, which every believer is meant to enjoy, or as Paul put it, *"newness of life,"* we have to first understand that it was all made possible by the death of Christ at Calvary's Cross. Let us say it again:

"For if we have been planted together in the likeness of His death, we shall be also in the likeness of His resurrection" (Rom. 6:5).

In other words, to have resurrection life, we must first of all understand that it is all made possible by our being *"planted together with Christ in the likeness of His death."*

Most definitely, the resurrection of Christ is of supreme significance, as should be obvious and well understood; however, it was not at the resurrection where our victory was won, but rather the Cross of Christ.

THE ATTACK AGAINST THE CROSS

I personally feel that a greater attack is being made presently against the Cross of Christ than ever before.

To be sure, Satan has always attacked the Cross, and for all the obvious reasons, but, heretofore, it has mostly been done by and through those who are unbelievers, such as the modernists, etc. However, this attack presently is from those who claim to be Spirit-filled, and I speak of the Word of Faith people, etc.

They refer to the Cross as "past miseries." They also call it "the greatest defeat in human history." They claim that if the preacher preaches the Cross, he is preaching death. They then go on and encourage their people to place their faith in the resurrection or the exaltation of Christ. However, what does the Bible say?

THE WORD OF GOD

Paul said, *"For Christ sent me not to baptize, but to preach the Gospel: not with wisdom of words, lest the Cross of Christ should be made of none effect"* (I Cor. 1:17).

He did not say, "Lest the resurrection or the exaltation of Christ should be made of none effect."

The great apostle also said, *"For the preaching of the Cross is to them who perish foolishness; but unto us who are saved it is the power of God"* (I Cor. 1:18).

He did not say, "For the preaching of the resurrection."

He said, *"But we preach Christ crucified"* (I Cor. 1:23).

He did not say, at least as it regarded salvation and sanctification, "But we preach Christ resurrected."

He also said, *"For I determined not to know anything among you, save Jesus Christ, and Him crucified"* (I Cor. 2:2).

He did not say, "For I determined not to know anything among you, save Jesus Christ and Him resurrected."

He said, *"But God forbid that I should glory, save in the Cross of our Lord Jesus Christ"* (Gal. 6:14).

He did not say, "But God forbid that I should glory, save in the resurrection of our Lord Jesus Christ."

MADE POSSIBLE BY THE CROSS

No, the great apostle was not denigrating the resurrection or the exaltation of Christ in any way, and neither are we. These things mentioned are of tremendous significance, as should be obvious; however, the resurrection of Christ and the exaltation of Christ before the Father were all made possible by what He did at the Cross. If Christ had not carried out a full atonement, thereby, defeating all the powers of darkness, and for all time, there would have been no resurrection, etc. In fact, if there had been one sin left unatoned, Jesus could not have risen from the dead. The reason is, *"The wages of sin is death"* (Rom. 6:23).

Now, you can believe the Word of God, of which we have just given you ample proof, or you can believe these preachers who are denigrating the Cross. Also, there is one other thing that the Apostle Paul said about those who would denigrate the Cross:

"But though we, or an angel from heaven, preach any other gospel unto you than that which we have preached unto you, let him be accursed" (Gal. 1:8).

THE FORMULA

Actually, as it regards living a victorious life in Christ, there is no formula as we think of such; however, perhaps the following might be of help. In fact, I know it will be of help if you will read it carefully and begin to practice it in your life.

- THE SOURCE: Jesus Christ is the source of all things that we receive from God (Jn. 1:1-3, 14, 29; 14:6; Col. 2:10-15).

- THE MEANS: The Cross of Christ is the means by which all of these things are given to us. Without the Cross, there would be no salvation, no baptism with the Holy Spirit, no divine healing, and no communion with the Lord. Everything is made possible by the Cross (Rom. 6:1-14; Gal. 6:14).

- OBJECT OF FAITH: Inasmuch as the Cross of Christ is the means by which all things are given to us, then the Cross of Christ, or we might say, Christ and Him crucified, must be the object of our faith. In fact, the entirety of the story of the Bible, all the way from Genesis 1:1 through Revelation 22:21, is the story of Christ and Him crucified.

- THE HOLY SPIRIT: The Holy Spirit works exclusively within the parameters, so to speak, of the finished work of Christ. In other words, it is the Cross that gives the Holy Spirit the latitude to do all that He does. In fact, the Holy Spirit can little work outside of the Cross, if at all (Rom. 8:1-11; Eph. 2:13-18).

THE LORD'S APPEARANCE TO SOLOMON

And the LORD appeared to Solomon by night, and said unto him, I have heard your prayer, and have chosen this place to Myself for an house of sacrifice. If I shut up heaven that there be no rain, or if I command the locusts to devour the land, or if I send pestilence among My people; If My people, who are called by My name, shall humble themselves, and pray, and seek My face, and turn from their wicked ways; then will I hear from heaven, and will forgive their sin, and will heal their land. Now My eyes shall be open, and My ears attent unto the prayer that is made in this place. For now have I chosen and sanctified this house, that My name may be there forever:

and My eyes and My heart shall be there perpetually. And as for you, if you will walk before Me, as David your father walked, and do according to all that I have commanded you, and shall observe My statutes and My judgments; Then will I stablish the throne of your kingdom, according as I have covenanted with David your father, saying, There shall not fail you a man to be ruler in Israel. But if you turn away, and forsake My statutes and My commandments, which I have set before you, and shall go and serve other gods, and worship them; Then will I pluck them up by the roots out of My land which I have given them; and this house, which I have sanctified for My name, will I cast out of My sight, and will make it to be a proverb and a byword among all nations. And this house, which is high, shall be an astonishment to everyone who passes by it; so that he shall say, Why has the LORD *done thus unto this land, and unto this house? And it shall be answered, Because they forsook the* LORD *God of their fathers, which brought them forth out of the land of Egypt, and laid hold on other gods, and worshipped them, and served them: therefore has He brought all this evil upon them* (II Chron. 7:12-22).

FIRE FROM HEAVEN

The Lord not only answered Solomon's prayer by a manifestation of the fire falling from heaven, but, as well, He portrayed in no uncertain terms what He would do as it regarded Solomon's petition. Also, we find here that the Lord referred to the temple as a *"house of sacrifice."* We should take note that the modern church should fall into the same category inasmuch as our message should be Jesus Christ and Him crucified (I Cor. 1:23).

The Cross must be the primary message (Rom. 6:3-14; I Cor. 2:2). It was there, the Cross, where all sin was atoned, meaning that the sin debt is no longer in the heart and life of those who trust Christ. As well, at the Cross, Satan, plus every other fallen angel and every demon spirit, were totally and completely defeated. In verse 14, *"If My people ... "* constitutes a prayer of repentance and, thereby, proclaims the manner of true repentance.

Prayer from a distance being made toward the temple would be answered. Due to what Christ did at the Cross, the Lord no longer resides in a building, but rather in the hearts and lives of all believers (I Cor. 3:16).

Now, instead of praying toward the east or wherever, we pray to the Father in heaven, and do so in the name of Jesus (Jn. 16:23).

Verses 19 through 22 portray the Solomonic covenant, which was conditional. In other words, if Solomon or his sons forsook the Lord, the Lord would forsake them.

These two covenants basically proclaim the correct scriptural teaching on predestination. It was predestined that God would have a nation called Israel (the Davidic covenant). Man's acceptance, rejection, failure, or otherwise did not alter the fact; however, who will actually be a part of the Israel that is saved (the Solomonic covenant) will depend on obedience. Actually, Paul said only a remnant would be saved (Rom. 9:27).

HOUSE OF SACRIFICE

Despite the fact that the temple was the most costly structure in the world, still, the Holy Spirit alluded to it rather as a *"house of sacrifice."* Despite the fact that there was more gold in this building than any other structure in the world, the Holy Spirit still made no mention of that whatsoever, again referring to the temple as a *"house of sacrifice."* Despite the fact that everything carried on in this house was of supreme significance, still, the Holy Spirit referred to it as a *"house of sacrifice,"* which referred to the real purpose of this structure.

As we have said and will continue to say, the Cross of Christ is the foundation of the entirety of the plan of God, actually formulated in the mind of the Godhead from before the foundation of the world (I Pet. 1:18-20).

While all the other things that pertain to the Lord are vastly significant, as should be obvious, still, it is the Cross of Christ that is at the very center and circumference of the plan of God.

In other words, every other doctrine, every other principle, and every other premise, all and without exception must be built upon the foundation of the Cross. If that is not the case, error will be the result, which means that God cannot bless it. He can only bless that which has the Cross of Christ as its foundation, and its foundation alone!

THE BRAZEN ALTAR

All of this means that the great brazen altar—30 feet long and 30 feet wide—which sat immediately in front of the temple, was in use 24 hours a day. Actually, the fires on that altar were to never go out. As well, the four horns that protruded from the altar, and did so from each corner, pointed to all points of the compass, telling us that what Jesus would do at the Cross would be for the entirety of the world (Jn. 3:16). This means that this great Gospel is for the entirety of mankind. It shows no preference or prejudice as it regards skin color, nationality, or creed. Jesus died for all! In fact, in the mind of God, there are only two races of people in this world—those who are saved and those who aren't.

If it is to be noticed, the answer that the Lord gave to Solomon began with the Cross of Christ, i.e., *"the house of sacrifice."*

THE ELEMENTS

In verse 13, the Holy Spirit plainly portrays to us that God rules all. He has the power to shut up heaven that there be no rain and the power to open heaven that there be copious showers. He can command the insects to *"devour the land,"* or He can give abundant crops. As well, He can send pestilence and sickness among the people, or He can stop it from coming to the people.

All of this means that anything and everything that happens to a child of God is either caused or allowed by the Lord.

While, of course, the Lord never causes sin, if a person is dead set upon committing sin, the Lord will allow such, but as always, the end result of sin is never pretty. In fact, all sin, in one way or the other, is a form of insanity. Even though the Lord will forgive and do so instantly, still, there is a price to pay for disobedience.

THE PRAYER OF REPENTANCE

- *"If My people"*: Even though this is an Old Testament prayer, still, it is just as valid presently as it was then. Sadly and unfortunately, at times, God's people stray from the Word of God. When they do, all types of problems occur.

- *"Humble themselves"*: How hard is it for one to humble oneself before the Lord? It's not hard at all, but yet, it seems to be an overwhelming factor in the lives of many, if not most. Pride is the problem, and that's why the Lord demands humility. We have to humble ourselves before Him and admit that we are wrong and that He alone holds the solution and, in fact, is the solution.

- *"Pray and seek My face"*: The believer, and we are speaking of believers here, should know how to pray. If it is to be noticed, the Lord did not tell us to consult a psychologist or even to seek counseling. He told us to *"pray and seek His face."*

- *"Turn from your wicked ways"*: That is what repentance is all about. It is turning from something, in this case sin, and turning to something, which is presently the Lord Jesus Christ.

Since the Cross, the believer is to repent not only of the evil that he or she has done but, as well, even the good. What do we mean by that?

REPENT OF THE GOOD AS WELL AS THE EVIL?

We tend to think that doing good will solve the problem, whatever the good might be. It won't! That's what Jesus meant when He told us to deny ourselves (Lk. 9:23). He was referring to denying our ability, strength, intellect, motivation, education, personal power, talent, etc.

We are to look exclusively to Him and what He did for us at the Cross. In other words, we are to depend totally on Christ and His sacrificial atoning work.

- *"Then will I hear from heaven"*: If we do it God's way, He has promised to hear us. To be sure, if He promised such under the old covenant, don't you think that He most definitely will do the same under the new covenant, especially considering that we now have an even better covenant, based on better promises (Heb. 8:6)?

- *"I will forgive their sin, and will heal their land"*: That's about as simple as it can get. If we will do what the Lord says do, to be sure, He most definitely will keep His promise without fail.

THE EYES AND EARS OF GOD

The Lord here said that He would be careful to *"see"* and to *"hear"* the *"prayer that is made in this place,"* referring to the temple. To those who truly desire to carry out the will of God, such presents itself as a great blessing.

To know that the Lord is watching us and listening for our prayers and petitions should be a tremendous consolation to all true believers. His eyes are open to see and to do, while His ears are open to be attentive to our praise, our prayer, and our petitions.

SANCTIFICATION OF THE HOUSE

Sanctification refers to being set apart, in this case, totally for the Lord. In other words, this house was to be separated from the world unto God. It is the same presently with believers.

If the believer is totally given over to the Lord, which refers more than anything else to his faith being placed entirely and totally within the Cross of Christ, then we have the promise that the eyes and the heart of the Lord will be on us perpetually (I Cor. 3:16).

THE CONDITIONS

David was ever used, as here, as the example.

Why?

How?

Considering the terrible sins that David committed—adultery with Bath-sheba and then murdering her husband in cold blood—how could this be?

While David definitely committed these terrible sins, the truth is, he paid dearly for what he did. In fact, he suffered an agony that was unimaginable. However, David's position with the Lord was not because of such suffering but because he truly repented of such actions, and as he always did, truly tried to follow the Lord as far as *"His statutes and judgments"* were concerned.

If Solomon would follow the Lord as did David his father, the Lord most definitely would keep His promises, with the throne of Israel being established, and, as well, the lineage of David continuing until the Messiah. Those were the conditions.

DESTRUCTION!

However, if Solomon and those who followed him would turn away from God and *"serve other gods, and worship them,"* the Lord also stated that He would decimate the throne of Israel and would, as well, destroy this house.

Unfortunately, with some few exceptions, the kings of Israel, although in the lineage of David, turned their backs on God and did exactly what the Lord told them not to do, which was to worship idols. To be sure, the Lord sent prophet after prophet unto them, seeking to turn them from their wicked ways, but it was all to no avail. So, the time finally came that the Lord was forced to do exactly what He said He would do, which was to forsake the nation and, thereby, allow the heathen to take it over, which Nebuchadnezzar did. It was all *"because they forsook the* L ORD *God of their fathers, which brought them forth out of the land of Egypt, and laid hold on other gods, and worshipped them, and served them."*

Let it be understood that the Lord, even under this dispensation of grace, can abide sin no more now than He could then. In fact, I think it can be said that He can abide it even less. The reasons ought to be obvious.

IGNORANCE?

Concerning this, Paul said, and I quote from The Expositor's Study Bible:

And the times of this ignorance God winked at (does not reflect that such ignorance was salvation, for it was not! before the Cross, there was very little light in the world, so God withheld judgment)*; but now commands all men everywhere to repent* (but since the Cross, the 'way' is open to all; it's up to us believers to make that 'way' known to all men)*: Because He has appointed a day* (refers to the coming of the great white throne judgment [Rev. 20:11-15])*, in the which*

He will judge the world in righteousness by that Man whom He has ordained (this righteousness is exclusively in Christ Jesus and what He has done for us at the Cross, and can be gained only by faith in Him [Eph. 2:8-9; Rom. 10:9-10, 13; Rev. 22:17]); *whereof He has given assurance unto all men, in that He has raised Him from the dead* (this refers to the resurrection ratifying that which was done at Cavalry and is applicable to all men, at least all who will believe) (Acts 17:30-31) (The Expositor's Study Bible)!

In other words, due to the Cross, the world has much less excuse now than at any time in human history. So, I think it can be said that even though the Lord promises much, much more under the new covenant, at the same time, He expects more from the church.

Hark! Ten thousand harps and voices
Sound the note of praise above;
Jesus reigns and heaven rejoices,
Jesus reigns, the God of love:
See He sits on yonder throne;
Jesus rules the world alone.

REFERENCES

CHAPTER 2

Chambers, Oswald. 1986. *My Utmost for His Highest: Selections for the Year.* Grand Rapids, MI: Oswald Chambers Publications; Marshall Pickering.

Williams, George. *The Complete Bible Commentary.* Grand Rapids, MI, United States: Kregel Publications, U.S., 2008. Print. Pg. 233

CHAPTER 3

Williams, George. *The Complete Bible Commentary.* Grand Rapids, MI, United States: Kregel Publications, U.S., 2008. Print. Pg. 234

CHAPTER 6

Williams, George. *The Complete Bible Commentary.* Grand Rapids, MI, United States: Kregel Publications, U.S., 2008.

CHAPTER 9

Calvin, John, and John King. *John Calvin's Commentaries on Isaiah 1-16: Extended Annotated Edition*. N.p.: Jazzybee Verlag, 2012. Print.

St. John Vol. II. Ed. H. D. M. Spence-Jones. *The Pulpit Commentary*. London; New York: Funk & Wagnalls Company, 1909.

Williams, George. *The Complete Bible Commentary*. Grand Rapids, MI, United States: Kregel Publications, U.S., 2008.

CHAPTER 12

Williams, George. *The Complete Bible Commentary*. Grand Rapids, MI, United States: Kregel Publications, U.S., 2008. Print. Pg. 244

St. John Vol. II. Ed. H. D. M. Spence-Jones. *The Pulpit Commentary*. London; New York: Funk & Wagnalls Company, 1909.

Wood, D. R. W. and I. Howard Marshall. *New Bible Dictionary*. 3rd ed. Leicester, England; Downers Grove, IL: InterVarsity Press, 1996.

ABOUT EVANGELIST JIMMY SWAGGART

The Rev. Jimmy Swaggart is a Pentecostal evangelist whose anointed preaching and teaching has drawn multitudes to the Cross of Christ since 1955.

As an author, he has written more than 50 books, commentaries, study guides, and The Expositor's Study Bible, which has sold more than 3 million copies.

As an award-winning musician and singer, Brother Swaggart has recorded more than 50 gospel albums and sold nearly 16 million recordings worldwide.

For more than six decades, Brother Swaggart has channeled his preaching and music ministry through multiple media venues including print, radio, television and the Internet.

In 2010, Jimmy Swaggart Ministries launched its own cable channel, SonLife Broadcasting Network, which airs 24 hours a day to a potential viewing audience of more than 1 billion people around the globe.

Brother Swaggart also pastors Family Worship Center in Baton Rouge, Louisiana, the church home and headquarters of Jimmy Swaggart Ministries.

Jimmy Swaggart Ministries materials can be found at **www.jsm.org**.

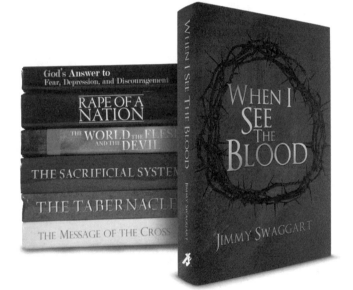